International Accounting Standards

From UK standards to IAS – an accelerated
route to understanding the key principles

Paul Rodgers

AMSTERDAM • BOSTON • HEIDELBERG • LONDON
NEW YORK • OXFORD • PARIS • SAN DIEGO
SAN FRANCISCO • SINGAPORE • SYDNEY • TOKYO

ELSEVIER

CIMA Publishing is an imprint of Elsevier

CIMA
PUBLISHING

CIMA Publishing is an imprint of Elsevier
Linacre House, Jordan Hill, Oxford OX2 8DP, UK
30 Corporate Drive, Suite 400, Burlington, MA 01803, USA

First edition 2007

Notice
No responsibility is assumed by the publisher for any injury and/or damage to persons
or property as a matter of products liability, negligence or otherwise, or from any use
or operation of any methods, products, instructions or ideas contained in the material
herein.

British Library Cataloguing in Publication Data
A catalogue record for this book is available from the British Library

978 0 7506 8203 9

For information on all CIMA publications
visit our website at books.elsevier.com

Typeset by Integra Software Services Pvt. Ltd, Pondicherry, India
www.integra-india.com

Printed and bound in Great Britain
07   08   09   10   10 9 8 7 6 5 4 3 2 1

Nothing is to be feared. It is only to be understood.

Marie Curie (1867–1934)

Contents

Introduction

The World never stands still and the same is true of the business community and the people that comprise it. Business organizations strive to improve their profits, borrow to fund growth or sell assets to facilitate survival, but the one thing they can never do is stand still or at least not for very long.

Furthermore the commercial universe comprises not of a meagre handful of business entities but millions ranging in size from the sole trader to the international conglomerate. If all of these factors are combined there appears to be a recipe for chaos, but this is not the case. As the number and complexity of business organizations has increased so have the rules and guidelines that constrain them.

The balance between these two forces is always a matter for debate with some commentators stating that the entrepreneurial spirit of business is being crushed by red tape, whilst others look for increased controls following a series of high profile corporate frauds such as WorldCom which required a $74.4 billion restatement of income. These rules come from many sources:

◆ Corporate legislation
◆ Industry guidelines
◆ Listing requirements and other stock exchange rules for public companies
◆ Accounting standards.

Let us focus on the larger corporations as these will be represented by household names with which we can all associate. These usually have a large and diverse investor base plus interactions with many other stakeholder groups ranging from suppliers/customers to government. The most readily available source of information on the business for all these user groups is the published financial statements, and it should come as no surprise that these have evolved from a simple historic record of transactions as seen 50 years ago to the detailed multi-part document seen today. Since the 1990s the evolution of financial statements has had three main strands.

1. *Corporate governance* There is a general principle that the management team of a company will enter into transactions that are in the best interests of the shareholders and other stakeholder groups.

Sadly the confidence of these stakeholders has been undermined by a series of high profile frauds and it was one of these, namely the financial mismanagement at the Enron Corporation, which initiated a groundswell for improved corporate governance.

The concept of corporate governance asks 'how well the managers manage', and has seen a tidal wave of new legislation and best practice rules instigated in all the major investment markets around the World. Most noteworthy of these has been the Sarbannes–Oxley Act in the USA and the Combined Code in the UK.

Disclosures relating to corporate governance and the audit of its compliance are now an integral feature of published accounts.

2. *Social and environmental reporting* Unlike corporate governance the majority of the rules on reporting how a business interacts with the environment are voluntary, but with increasing awareness of issues such as global warming and sustainability of resources this looks set to change.

The absence of statute initially created the danger that only those organizations that were perceived as environmentally aware would provide stakeholders with details of their policies. However, this is rapidly changing as it becomes apparent that socially aware policies can improve brand perception and hence add to shareholder value.

3. *International harmonization* With the development of the Internet, increased ease of international travel and the development of companies through international growth and acquisition, the days when an investor would usually be based in the same country as the business in which they had invested have passed. This brings huge opportunities but also creates a dilemma for a potential investor trying to appraise the relative merits of expanding their portfolio into new markets.

The accounting rules and conventions of different countries have been developed when little regard was needed for international consistency. This insular approach has now been found wanting on the global stage, and so the wheels were set in motion towards the harmonization of these divergent rules.

Of all the changes identified above it is the latter that has proved the most daunting with a natural instinct for the creators of national accounting rules to advocate their own work, and the logistics of changing local legislation.

However, the drive to harmonize accounting is often perceived as a technical exercise that will occupy the brains of accounting academics but have little real bearing on the average stakeholder. Hopefully the fact that you have picked up this book means that you are aware this is not the case, but if you have any lingering doubts let us take a snapshot of the evidence.

◆ Although harmonization is initially focussed on listed companies it has implications for businesses of every size either directly or indirectly through trading relationships.
◆ The reported performance and position of a business can be dramatically altered by the change to new accounting rules. Without an understanding of the main issues, investment appraisal could be seriously undermined.
◆ Providers of finance will need to review financial covenants included in funding agreements as the thresholds set may no longer be appropriate.

At this point you might be sensing a degree of trepidation envisaging the stacks of paperwork you need to read bulging with the technical jargon of accountants.

BUT

Fear not!

There is a sensible compromise between blissful ignorance and the finely tailored skills of a public company finance director – think what you really need.

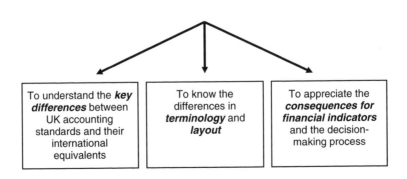

| To understand the **key differences** between UK accounting standards and their international equivalents | To know the differences in **terminology** and **layout** | To appreciate the **consequences for financial indicators** and the decision-making process |

The objective of this book is to provide a succinct and straightforward route map to meeting these needs. It will allow you to pick and choose subjects of particular interest or taken in aggregate provide a direct path to a big picture understanding of the consequences of the switch to international accounting — let us get to work!

Harmonization – The Story
So Far

A long winding road

Our priority is to understand the impact of the transition from UK to current international accounting rules on company financial statements, but this will be easier if we have an overview of the sequence of events that brought us to the brink of this groundbreaking transition.

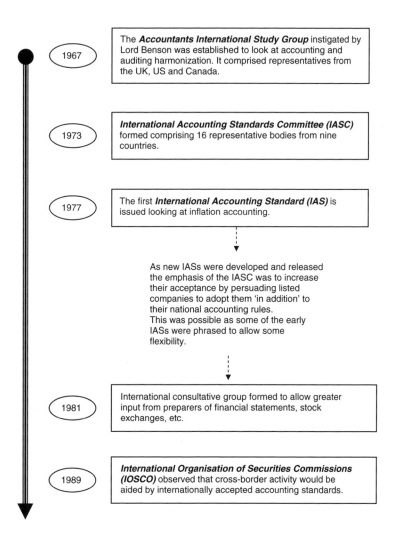

1967
The **Accountants International Study Group** instigated by Lord Benson was established to look at accounting and auditing harmonization. It comprised representatives from the UK, US and Canada.

1973
International Accounting Standards Committee (IASC) formed comprising 16 representative bodies from nine countries.

1977
The first **International Accounting Standard (IAS)** is issued looking at inflation accounting.

As new IASs were developed and released the emphasis of the IASC was to increase their acceptance by persuading listed companies to adopt them 'in addition' to their national accounting rules.
This was possible as some of the early IASs were phrased to allow some flexibility.

1981
International consultative group formed to allow greater input from preparers of financial statements, stock exchanges, etc.

1989
International Organisation of Securities Commissions (IOSCO) observed that cross-border activity would be aided by internationally accepted accounting standards.

1994

IOSCO reviewed existing international standards and identified changes it considered necessary before it would recommend their use in cross-border transactions.

By the early 1990s a change of emphasis had emerged from the IASC. With a significant number of standards now in issue they looked to:

- Strengthen existing standards
- Fill noteworthy gaps
- Try to eliminate inconsistencies with national rules

This was now given added impetus to meet the demands of IOSCO.

1995

Advisory Council formed comprising of leading figures from varied backgrounds to act as a sounding board for IASC decisions.

1997

Standings Interpretation Committee (SIC) formed to allow a rapid review of contentious areas or divergent views.

1999

The improvements and additional standards required by IOSCO were completed and put forward for its review. Although, not the original intention, IOSCO acceptance was now focussed on gaining acceptance from the US *Securities and Exchange Commission (SEC)*.

Many other leading exchanges including those of the European Union had already indicated their acceptance of using IAS for cross-border listings without requiring a reconciliation to national GAAP (Generally Accepted Accounting Practice). It was the need for such a reconciliation that created one of the greatest barriers to change because of the additional work it required from the preparers of financial information.

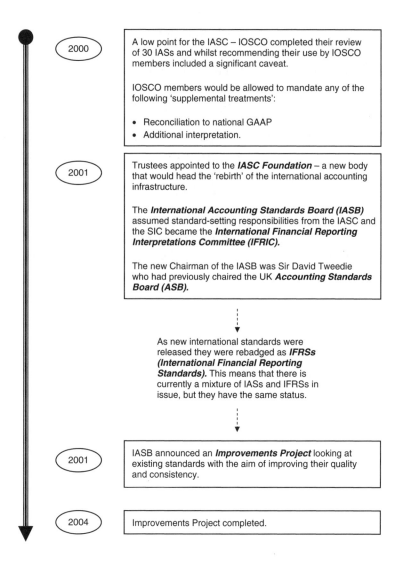

2000 A low point for the IASC – IOSCO completed their review of 30 IASs and whilst recommending their use by IOSCO members included a significant caveat.

IOSCO members would be allowed to mandate any of the following 'supplemental treatments':

- Reconciliation to national GAAP
- Additional interpretation.

2001 Trustees appointed to the *IASC Foundation* – a new body that would head the 'rebirth' of the international accounting infrastructure.

The *International Accounting Standards Board (IASB)* assumed standard-setting responsibilities from the IASC and the SIC became the *International Financial Reporting Interpretations Committee (IFRIC).*

The new Chairman of the IASB was Sir David Tweedie who had previously chaired the UK *Accounting Standards Board (ASB).*

As new international standards were released they were rebadged as *IFRSs (International Financial Reporting Standards).* This means that there is currently a mixture of IASs and IFRSs in issue, but they have the same status.

2001 IASB announced an *Improvements Project* looking at existing standards with the aim of improving their quality and consistency.

2004 Improvements Project completed.

2005 – The year when the accounting world would change forever

The member states of the European Union (EU) each have a rich social and economic history, and this extends to the development of national accounting best practice. However, this independent evolution creates challenges to the EU when trying to balance the retention of individual identity with the development of a single market that both encourages and reduces the costs of international trade between members.

The most common mechanism for creating uniformity has been the issue of Directives, which require member states to modify their national legislation to ensure compliance. This concept will be very familiar to accountants in the UK who have been effectively required to follow the EU Fourth and Seventh Directives.

Fourth Directive	Prescribes financial statement formats, note disclosures and provides rules on valuation
Seventh Directive	Prescribes rules for the preparation of consolidated financial statements

Some aspects of these Directives were undoubtedly compromises. This was not ideal but necessary to bridge some core conceptual differences between member states, the most noteworthy of which was the very purpose for which financial information was being created.

United Kingdom	Germany
Shareholders are perceived as the most important stakeholder in the receipt of financial information as historically they had been the biggest provider of finance	Financial statements are prepared for the tax authorities, and consequently the calculation of taxable profit

The EU recognized that, with aspirations to increase the number of member states, a more robust and comprehensive accounting legislation was required, and in 1995 acknowledged that closer liaison with the IASC and IOSCO was required to achieve this objective – the wheels of change had been set in motion albeit slowly.

It was not until 2000 that the European Commission announced proposals for all listed EU companies to produce financial statements complying with IAS by 2005. Suddenly the pace of change quickened with changes being made to the Fourth and Seventh Directives to avoid conflict with international accounting rules and in July 2002 the requirement for the adoption of international accounting rules became EU policy.

This decision set in motion a cascade of activity within the listed companies of the EU as they prepared their staff and systems for the changes ahead.

On 1 January 2007 Romania and Bulgaria increased the constituency of the EU to 27 member states, and with the prospect of further enlargement still to come the EU represents the showcase through which the IASB can bring international accounting to the forefront of the financial world.

The EU was not alone

The IASB continues to work actively towards the global acceptance of its accounting standards with approximately 100 countries indicating an intention to adopt IFRS or alter their national GAAP to make it compliant at the date of publication.

However, as with any transition of this magnitude the time scale and details of implementation differ markedly.

The spectrum of IFRS compliance as at January 2007

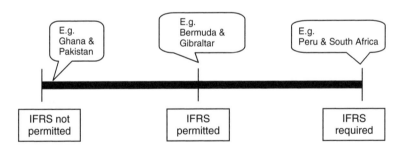

Convergence with US GAAP

Although the decision by IOSCO in 2000 not to give unqualified acceptance of IAS allowed the US SEC to require companies listing on a US exchange to provide a reconciliation with US GAAP this did not represent an accounting isolationist policy. This was confirmed in 2002 by the signing of the Norwalk Agreement between the IASB and the US Financial Accounting Standards Board (FASB), specifying an intention to work together in the development of accounting standards that facilitated the harmonization of US and international GAAP.

Immediate steps were taken to eliminate discrepancies where agreement was easily obtained, and a longer term but practical approach adopted to areas of greater disparity. This process is ongoing and may take until the end of Sir David Tweedie's second term as Chairman of the IASB (i.e. 2011).

Sadly this means that the necessity for non-US companies listing on the New York Stock Exchange or NASDAQ to prepare a reconciliation of profit and equity from IFRS to US GAAP remains.

Finance directors beware

Place yourself in the position of a finance director of a UK listed company, and consider how the business you represent interacts with the business world that surrounds it. The volume of change, both commercial and legislative, is staggering (Figure 1.1):

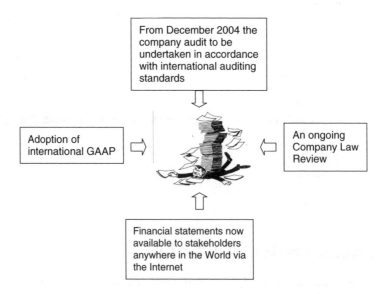

Figure 1.1 The changing world of business

Change is inevitable but occasionally there is a need to pause for breath otherwise there is a danger of focus moving disproportionately from business success to compliance and this is not in the best interests of any stakeholder group. The IASB have recognized this and in 2006 steps were taken to achieve this objective.

◆ One year will be allowed between the date of publication of a wholly new IFRS or major amendment to existing IFRSs and the date when implementation is required.
◆ No new standards to be effective before 2008, and in line with this move the application of new IFRSs under development will not require implementation until 1 January 2009.

Let us not lose sight of the benefits

There is always resistance to change and numerous commentators have observed that they do not believe the cost of transition to IFRS is offset by measurable benefits. It is certainly true that the cost of computer infrastructure and the marginal cost of key staff has been high, particularly in financial institutions. Additionally the financial position and performance of companies immediately post-transition has not been one of consistent improvement or deterioration, but has been heavily dependent on which accounting standards are most significant to a particular business.

The true benefits are longer term, but this does not make them any less desirable.

1. Increased disclosures will improve the transparency of financial statements.
2. Comparability remains the biggest benefit in a global market, and it will only be when the harmonization process is completed with the US that the ultimate prize will be reached.
3. The ability of a company to communicate with all stakeholder groups will be improved.
4. The cost of capital will fall and market liquidity improve.

Key Facts

1. Global harmonization of accounting best practice has been evolving since the 1960s but has seen a sharp acceleration as we enter the 21st century.
2. The International Accounting Standards Board is the leading organization in the harmonization process.

3. The US remains the largest financial market resistant to the recognition of IFRS, but following the 2002 Norwalk Agreement the IASB and their US equivalent, the FASB, are working together towards a long-term solution.

4. EU listed companies producing group financial statements must adopt international GAAP from 2005 (for more on this, see Chapter 2).

5. Large companies have been faced with an ever-increasing wave of change extending beyond the requirements of the IASB to company law and audit regulations. The IASB has recognized the need for a breathing space so that systems can be implemented and stakeholders given the opportunity to familiarize themselves with the changes.

6. The long-term benefits of global harmonization of accounting practice are immense – it is very much a case of short-term pain for long-term gain.

The Mechanics of Transition

Which UK companies have had to make the transition to IFRS?

The basic rule is:

> **All listed companies in the EU have to prepare their consolidated financial statements in accordance with International Financial Reporting Standards for financial years starting on or after 1 January 2005**

Let us analyse the practicalities in more detail.

1. *Exact timing* Although early adoption was permitted for those companies following the EU regulation the earliest to make the transition will have been those with a 31 December 2005 year end as this will have been the first full financial year completed after the mandatory date. Companies with different year ends will have transferred at their respective year ends in 2006 (Figure 2.1).

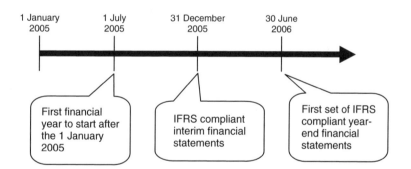

Figure 2.1 Transition date to IFRS for a UK company with a 30 June year end

2. *Listed companies* The rules apply to any company that has shares or debt traded on a regulated market in any of the EU regulated states. Consequently this covers not only the London Stock Exchange but organizations such as LIFFE (The London International Financial Futures and Options Exchange).

Although this appears to give very broad coverage it does not include AIM as this ceased to be a regulated market prior to 1 January 2005. This does not mean that companies listed in this market escape the net, but in recognition of their smaller size they have been given a

2-year extension, and do not need to comply until after 1 January 2007. This dispensation helps ensure that disproportionate resources are not required to facilitate the transition.

It should be noted that companies governed by the laws of a non-member state fall outside the EU regulation and consequently do not have to apply IFRS although it is possible that individual exchanges may toughen up their own rule book to require this in the future.

3. *Consolidated financial statements*   The regulation only applies to the consolidated financial statements of a business, but there was an anticipation by the IASB that this would cascade down to the individual financial statements of the constituent companies. This appears logical as it would make the process of preparing group figures much easier, and facilitate stronger systems and controls within the business. In the UK this has been further strengthened by the Government which has implemented a restriction only allowing divergent GAAP if there is 'good reason'.

Under the EU regulation a parent company is allowed to elect to continue to prepare its own financial statements using national GAAP, and there are occasions when this can appear attractive. As we examine the impact of detailed changes to IFRS it will be observed that the resultant profits and reserves of a business might increase or decrease and it is the latter that might persuade a company not to adopt IFRS at the non-group level. Remember that dividends are legally paid by individual companies and not by groups, and so the maximization of distributable reserves could lead to this dichotomy of accounting treatment.

How a company validates 'good reason' for such divergent treatment in the UK waits to be fully tested!

If a company falls outside the scope of the regulations there is no requirement for it to transfer to the use of IFRS although EU Member States are allowed to extend the requirement if they consider it desirable. In the UK it remains optional, with the exception of charitable companies that are not currently allowed to use IFRS, but you should be aware that the tide is running in one direction.

◆ Following the application of IFRS a company cannot revert to UK GAAP except under restricted circumstances such as its debt/equity ceasing to be listed on a regulated market.

- Companies with ambitions to list on a regulated market have a strong incentive to change.
- UK accounting standards are progressively being updated and this effectively involves the adoption of the relevant IAS/IFRS subject to modest adjustments to reflect idiosyncrasies in the law or accepted UK practice. Eventually a company professing to use UK GAAP will effectively be using international GAAP.

The small company conundrum

Without a capital market focus the costs of transition to IFRS can appear daunting, and the smaller the business the greater the perceived disparity between cost and reward.

In the UK this problem becomes starker if we look a little deeper at the major components of UK GAAP.

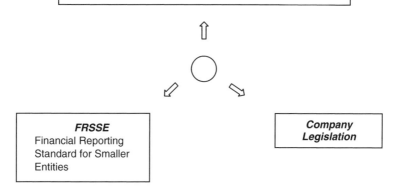

UK Accounting Standards
As with their international counterparts there are two labels for UK standards following a name change as new versions were released.

1. SSAPs – Statement of Standard Accounting Practice (older standards)
2. FRSs – Financial Reporting Standard (from 1991 onwards)

FRSSE
Financial Reporting Standard for Smaller Entities

Company Legislation

At 1 January 2007 the UK company legislation categorized a company as small or medium-sized if it met the following criteria:

- A company is not eligible for any of the exemptions if it is
  - A public company
  - A banking or insurance company

- An authorized person under the Financial Services Act 1986
- A member of an ineligible group (i.e. a group containing any of the above).

◆ Any two of the three criteria must be met or have been met in the previous year.

Criteria	Small Company	Medium Company
Turnover	£5.6 million	£22.8 million
Balance sheet total	£2.8 million	£11.4 million
Number of employees	50 employees	250 employees

The Companies Act 1985 allows disclosure dispensations in their published accounts for both small and medium-sized companies, but companies that qualify as small are also allowed to use the FRSSE in preference to the full suite of accounting standards. This is potentially very attractive to a small company finance director as it allows them to sidestep the complexities of mainstream standards which would be inappropriate to their needs.

The FRSSE brings together the accounting requirements and disclosures from other accounting standards that are appropriate to small businesses, and is regularly revised to ensure that it reflects current best practice.

NOTE: The FRSSE also reflects releases by the Urgent Issues Task Force (UITF) or areas where specific guidance was needed on application of a broader standard.

Under current international GAAP there is no equivalent to the FRSSE, meaning that small companies switching to this regime would be required to apply the full suite of international standards. This would appear a very onerous task to a management team currently employing the FRSSE.

The IASB are aware of this issue and have been working on an equivalent standard for Small and Medium Sized Entities (SMEs).

It is anticipated that this document will be finally approved in 2007–08, and will be received with great interest by the business community.

First-time adoption: The basics

The IASB recognized that the transition from national GAAP to IFRS required specific guidance to be provided to businesses, and towards this end they issued a standard uniquely focussed on this subject. IFRS 1 *First-time Adoption of International Financial Reporting Standards* is a comprehensive document designed to ensure that the first IFRS compliant accounts, interim or year end, prepared by a company contained high quality information that:

◆ Is transparent and comparable over all periods presented
◆ Gives a good starting point for using IFRS
◆ Can be produced at a cost that does not exceed the benefit to users

[IFRS 1 para 1]

IFRS 1 makes it clear that first-time adoption is not for the faint-hearted, and requires the company to make an explicit and unreserved statement of compliance with IFRS.

With 2005–06 now representing history you might consider that the significance of this standard to your understanding is limited, but this is not the case. The consequences of transition impact our ability to interpret and analyse the position and performance of the business in later years. Figure 2.2 examines what first-time adoption means for a company with a 31 December 2005 year end.

All adjustments required to move from UK GAAP to IFRS at the time of first adoption had to be recognized directly in retained earnings.

Departure from the retrospective application of IFRS shown in Figure 2.2 was allowed only under restricted circumstances where it could be shown that it was too difficult, resulting in an adverse cost–benefit or leading to the use of hindsight. IFRS 1 identified a small number of mandatory and optional exemptions and these will be considered later in the text after we have seen the impact of the consequences of mainstream transition.

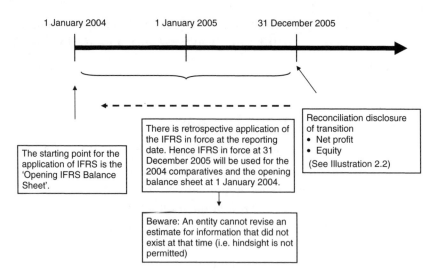

Figure 2.2 Overview of the mechanics of transition to IFRS for a company with a 31 December 2005 year end

---

Box 2.1 Example of IFRS transition reconciliation disclosure – Laura Ashley Holdings plc (2006)

28. reconciliation of profit for the 52 weeks ended 29 January 2005

	UK GAAP £m	*effect of transition* £m	IFRS £m
Revenue	238.9	–	238.9
Cost of sales	(137.9)	–	(137.9)
Gross profit	101.0	–	101.0
Operating expenses	(96.2)	(0.1)	(96.3)
Profit from operations	4.8	(0.1)	4.7
Share of operating profit of associate	0.4	–	0.4
Net financing cost	(0.4)	(0.3)	(0.7)
Profit before taxation	4.8	(0.4)	4.4
Taxation	(1.3)	–	(1.3)
Profit for the financial year	3.5	(0.4)	3.1

The impact of the transition to IFRS is an increase in the net operating expenses and net financing costs of £0.1 million and £0.3 million respectively.

30. reconciliation of net assets as at 29 January 2005

	UK GAAP £m	effect of transition £m	IFRS £m
Non-current assets			
Property, plant and equipment	31.9	–	31.9
Deferred tax asset	–	3.9	3.9
Investment in associate	3.5	–	3.5
	35.4	3.9	39.3
Current assets			
Inventories	34.9	–	34.9
Trade and other receivables	23.1	–	23.1
Cash and cash equivalents	16.1	–	16.1
	74.1	–	74.1
Total assets	109.5	3.9	113.4
Current liabilities			
Current tax liabilities	2.0	–	2.0
Bank borrowings	0.9	–	0.9
Obligations under finance leases	0.3	–	0.3
Trade and other payables	36.7	–	36.7
	39.9	–	39.9
Non-current liabilities			
Bank borrowings	4.6	–	4.6
Obligations under finance leases	0.5	–	0.5
Retirement benefit obligations	–	13.3	13.3
Provisions and other liabilities	0.2	–	0.2
	5.3	13.3	18.6
Total liabilities	45.2	13.3	58.5
Net assets	64.3	(9.4)	54.9

The impact of implementing IAS 19 is to recognise a pension liability of £13.3 million in the Group's Balance Sheet. The net impact is a reduction in the consolidated net assets of £9.4 million after deducting the related deferred tax of £3.9 million.

The transition to IFRS has a wide ranging impact on the numbers shown in the financial statements.

- ◆ Derecognition of some assets and liabilities shown under UK GAAP
- ◆ Recognition of new assets and liabilities
- ◆ Reclassification
- ◆ Changed measurement.

It is our mission to now examine these consequences in detail and understand the impact they have had on the financial information placed before us.

Key Facts

1. EU regulated listed companies had to transfer the basis of their financial statement preparation to IFRS for accounting periods starting on or after 1 January 2005.
2. Application is retrospective and requires restatement of comparatives using IFRS in application at the date of transition.
3. Small companies currently using the FRSSE will await the introduction of a new IFRS dedicated to small and medium sized entities.
4. AIM listed companies have been given a 2-year extension to the implementation date.

The Conceptual Framework

The Christmas tree approach

When the Christmas festive season arrives and decorated spruce trees abound do you ever ask what is supporting the multi-coloured baubles and lights?

I doubt that you do as we simply take pleasure in the overall effect not consciously acknowledging the branches of the tree supporting this display. The Conceptual Framework of the IASB shares this attribute in that it is rarely a focal point when analysing financial statements and yet it is at the heart of every accounting standard ensuring consistency of terminology, recognition and measurement.

Every major GAAP has a conceptual core:

◆ International GAAP = The Conceptual Framework
◆ UK GAAP = The Statement of Principles
◆ US GAAP = Conceptual Framework.

In 2006 the FASB and IASB issued a consultative document setting out their preliminary views on the first two chapters of a unified Conceptual Framework, marking another step in the progress towards a single global accounting rule set. However, the differences between the existing conceptual documents is quite modest as can be seen from a broad comparison of the subjects covered by the main chapters/sections of the UK and international versions (Table 3.1).

Table 3.1 Comparison of main elements of the UK's Statement of Principles and the IASB's Accounting Framework

The Conceptual Framework	Chapter/Sections	The Statement of Principles
The objective of financial statements	1	The objective of financial statements
Underlying assumptions	2	The reporting entity
Qualitative characteristics of financial statements	3	The qualitative characteristics of financial information
The elements of financial statements	4	The elements of financial statements
Recognition of the elements of financial statements	5	Recognition in financial statements
Measurement of the elements of financial statements	6	Measurement in financial statements
Concepts of capital and capital maintenance	7	Presentation of financial information
	8	Accounting for interests in other entities

The emphasis of this book is to look at UK GAAP and IFRS GAAP differences and similarities from a practical perspective, and hence we do not dwell on the conceptual backdrop, but to act as reference source Table 3.2 gives some additional details of terms and principles that derive from the Conceptual Framework.

Table 3.2 A synopsis of the Conceptual Framework

Section 1: The objective of financial statements	To provide information about the financial position, performance and changes in financial position of an enterprise that is useful to a wide range of users in making economic decisions
Section 2: Underlying assumptions	There are two such assumptions. 1 **The Accruals Basis of Accounting**: The effects of transactions are recognized when they occur, which may not be the same as when the cash flows 2 **Going Concern Basis**. Financial statements prepared on the assumption that the enterprise is a going concern.

Table 3.2 A synopsis of the Conceptual Framework—cont'd

Section 3: Qualitative characteristics of financial statements	◆ ***Understandability***
	◆ ***Relevance***
	  – Includes the concept of *materiality* – would omission or misstatement influence the economic decisions of financial statement users
	◆ ***Reliability***
	This incorporates:
	  – Neutrality
	  – Prudence
	  – Substance over form
	  – Completeness
	  – Faithful representation
	◆ ***Comparability***

Section 4: The elements of financial statements	This is a vital section as it defines terms that are often taken for granted. ***Asset***: A resource controlled by the enterprise as a result of past events and from which future economic benefits are expected to flow into the enterprise. ***Liability***: A present obligation of the enterprise arising from past events, the settlement of which is expected to result in the outflow from the enterprise of resources embodying economic benefits. ***Equity***: The residual interest in the assets of the enterprise after deducting all its liabilities. ***Income***: Increases in economic benefits during the accounting period in the form of inflows or enhancements of assets or decreases of liabilities that result in increases in equity, other than relating to contributions from equity participants. ***Expenses***: Decreases in economic benefits during the accounting period in the form of outflows or depletions of assets or occurrences of liabilities that result in decreases in equity, other than those relating to distributions to equity participants.
Section 5: Recognition of elements of financial statements	An asset will be recognized if it is probable that future economic benefits will flow to the enterprise and the asset has a cost or value that can be measured reliably. Similar principles apply to liabilities except that it is probable that resources embodying economic benefits will flow out from the enterprise.

25

Continued

Table 3.2 A synopsis of the Conceptual Framework—cont'd	
Section 6: Measurement of the elements of financial statements	This refers to the type of conceptual measurement that can be used and it identifies four. 1 Historic cost 2 Current cost 3 Realizable value 4 Present value
Section 7: Concepts of capital and capital maintenance	Two concepts of capital maintenance are identified. 1. *Financial Capital Maintenance*: where capital is synonymous with the net assets or equity of the enterprise. 2. *Physical Capital Maintenance*: where capital is regarded as the productive capacity of the enterprise.

Key Facts

1. The Conceptual Framework underpins every international accounting standard, and will act as a useful reference point for analysts when trying to understand unique or new transactions of an enterprise.

Presentation – The Big Picture

What to expect in financial statements prepared under IFRS

As a general principle the financial statements of listed companies are getting longer as they attempt to address the needs of a wider stakeholder group, address weaknesses highlighted by corporate frauds and appear responsive to the changing environment in which they operate.

Since the shock waves from the Enron fraud corporate governance, disclosures have gained more prominence and the increasing significance given to social and environmental awareness are featuring more prominently in management commentaries. However, do not believe that it is simply the other information issued with published accounts that is increasing as it is also the core product that is expanding and observers will particularly notice this in the transition to IFRS.

Under UK GAAP the accounts have comprised of four primary documents needed for a true and fair view to be given to the shareholders plus accounting policies and other notes needed for the clarification of the key numbers. When you first pick up a set of accounts prepared under IFRS you will notice some immediate differences without considering the detail.

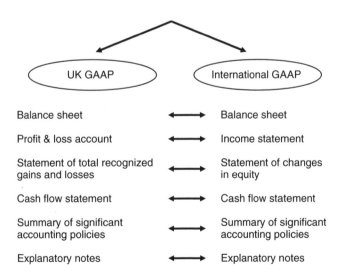

Do not be fooled into believing that because both systems use the same title that the detail will be the same – it is these differences we need to explore next.

Key Facts

1. The international equivalent to the profit and loss account is the income statement.
2. The international equivalent of the statement of total recognized gains and losses is the statement of changes in equity, but there are also some significant differences in detail.

Presentation – The Balance Sheet

Setting expectations

UK GAAP relating to balance-sheet presentation is based on prescriptive formats set out by company legislation, whereas international practice allows greater flexibility.

Illustrations

Box 5.1 J Sainsbury plc (2005) – UK GAAP

Balance sheets
at 26 March 2005 and 27 March 2004

	Note	Group 2005 £m	Group Restated 2004 £m	Company 2005 £m	Company Restated 2004 £m
Fixed assets					
Intangible assets	13	125	208	–	–
Tangible assets	14	7,154	8,214	330	361
Investments	15	20	30	9,122	8,109
		7,299	8,452	9,452	8,470
Current assets					
Stocks	18	559	753	–	–
Debtors					
Retail debtors (amounts falling due within one year)	19 z	271	319	29	14
Sainsbury's Bank debtors (amounts falling due within one year)	19	1,273	1,042	–	–
Sainsbury's Bank debtors (amounts falling due after more than one year)	19	1,342	1,170	–	–
		2,886	2,531	29	14
Assets held for resale	19	87	–	–	–
Investments	21	114	228	–	–
Cash at bank and in hand (including Sainsbury's Bank)	25	673	543	317	159
		4,319	4,055	346	173

	Note				
Creditors amounts falling due within one year					
Creditors					
Retail creditors	22	(2,152)	(2,197)	(2,607)	(837)
Sainsbury's Bank creditors	22	(2,555)	(2,279)	–	–
Borrowings	22	(4,707)	(4,476)	(2,607)	(837)
Sainsbury's Bank borrowings	23	(354)	(403)	(283)	(206)
	23	(36)	(27)	–	–
Net current liabilities		(778)	(851)	(2,544)	(870)
Total assets less current liabilities		6,521	7,601	6,908	7,600
Creditors amounts falling due after more than one year					
Creditors					
Retail creditors	22	(4)	(25)	(1,501)	(1,509)
Sainsbury's Bank creditors	22	(22)	–	–	–
Borrowings	22	(26)	(25)	(1,501)	(1,509)
	23	(1,704)	(2,169)	(1,704)	(1,868)
Provisions for liabilities and charges	26	(332)	(308)	(46)	(29)
Total net assets		4,459	5,099	3,657	4,194
Capital and reserves					
Called up share capital	27	620	486	620	486
Share premium account	27	761	1,438	761	1,438
Capital redemption reserve	28	547	–	547	–
Revaluation reserve	28	22	22	–	–
Profit and loss account	29	2,424	3,072	1,729	2,270
Total shareholders' funds (including non-equity interests)		4,374	5,018	3,657	4,194
Equity minority interest		85	81	–	–
Total capital employed		4,459	5,099	3,657	4,194

Box 5.2 J Sainsbury plc (2006) – International GAAP

Balance sheets

at 25 March 2006 and 26 March 2005

		Group		Company	
		2006	2005	2006	2005
	Note	£m	£m	£m	£m
Non-current assets					
Property, plant and equipment	12	7,060	7,076	251	330
Intangible assets	13	191	203	–	–
Investments	14	10	20	7,231	5,770
Available-for-sale financial assets	17	113	–	–	–
Amounts due from Sainsbury's Bank customers	16b	1,473	1,331	–	–
Other receivables	16a	–	–	1,751	368
Deferred income tax asset	22	55	–	7	–
		8,902	8,630	9,240	6,468
Current assets					
Inventories	15	576	559	–	–
Trade and other receivables	16a	276	319	150	2,885
Amounts due from Sainsbury's Bank customers and other banks	16b	1,888	1,227	–	–
Available-for-sale financial assets	17	52	–	–	–
Investments	18	–	90	–	–
Cash and cash equivalents	28b	1,028	706	411	317
		3,820	2,901	561	3,202
Non-current assets held for sale	19	25	87	–	–
		3,845	2,988	561	3,202
Total assets		12,747	11,618	9,801	9,670

Current liabilities					
Trade and other payables	20a	(2,094)	(2,093)	(5,119)	(2,483)
Amounts due to Sainsbury's Bank customers and other banks	20b	(2,299)	(2,464)	–	–
Short-term borrowings	21	(253)	(354)	(233)	(283)
Derivative financial instruments	31a	(10)	–	(10)	–
Taxes payable		(63)	(55)	9	(29)
Provisions	23	(91)	(70)	(2)	(13)
		(4,810)	(5,036)	(5,355)	(2,808)
Net current (liabilities)/assets		(965)	(2,048)	(4,794)	394
Non-current liabilities					
Other payables	20a	(30)	(31)	(782)	(1,501)
Amounts due to Sainsbury's Bank customers and other banks	20b	(1,009)	(22)	–	–
Long-term borrowings	21	(2,178)	(1,793)	–	(1,704)
Derivative financial instruments	31a	(2)	–	(2)	–
Deferred income tax liability	22	–	(1)	–	–
Provisions	23	(95)	(87)	(31)	(33)
Retirement benefit obligations	32	(658)	(536)	–	–
		(3,972)	(2,470)	(815)	(3,238)
Net assets		3,965	4,112	3,631	3,624
Equity					
Called up share capital	24	489	620	489	620
Share premium account	24	782	761	782	761
Capital redemption reserve	25	668	547	668	547
Other reserves	25	(1)	87	–	–
Retained earrings	26	1,948	2,012	1,692	1,696
Equity shareholders' funds	27	3,886	4,027	3,631	3,624
Minority interests	27	79	85	–	–
Total equity	27	3,965	4,112	3,631	3,624

Key differences

General layout

Schedule 4 of the UK Companies Act 1985 prescribes two formats for the balance sheet of a company. When a format has been selected the company must continue to use this for subsequent years unless the directors can justify special reasons for a change. Departure from the prescribed format is only allowed under very restricted circumstances:

◆ Required for the accounts to give a true and fair view
◆ Immaterial items can be disregarded
◆ Certain information can be given in the notes to the financial statements rather than on the face of the balance sheet itself
◆ Certain of the prescribed headings can be combined.

> NOTE: It is always possible to give more disclosure than that required.

Format 1 also referred to as the vertical presentation is the most common, whereas Format 2 presents information horizontally showing a total for assets on one side and a total for liabilities and equity on the other.

Internationally presentation cannot be prescribed by legislation as by definition it extends beyond national borders. Guidance on presentation comes from an accounting standard (IAS 1 *Presentation of Financial Statements*). This allows much greater flexibility although it does stipulate minimum disclosures that must be shown on the face of the statement and not in the notes. These minimum disclosures are

◆ Property, plant and equipment
◆ Investment property
◆ Intangible assets
◆ Financial assets
◆ Investments accounted for using the equity method
◆ Biological assets
◆ Inventories
◆ Trade and other receivables
◆ Cash and cash equivalents
◆ Trade and other payables

- ◆ Provisions
- ◆ Financial liabilities
- ◆ Liabilities and assets for current tax
- ◆ Deferred tax assets and deferred tax liabilities
- ◆ Minority interest
- ◆ Issued capital and reserves.

By reference to Boxes 5.1 and 5.2 it can be seen that the international balance-sheet presentation shows assets in the top section and liabilities plus equity in the bottom. However, the example also demonstrates that some companies will effectively give a hybrid presentation to facilitate stakeholder understanding; in this instance still giving a sub-total for net assets and showing liabilities prior to equity.

Terminology

It will also be apparent that certain terminology varies between the different systems.

UK GAAP		International GAAP
Fixed assets	=	Non-current assets
Tangible assets	=	Property, plant and equipment
Stocks	=	Inventories
Debtors	=	Receivables
Creditors	=	Payables
Creditors falling due within 1 year	=	Current liabilities
Creditors falling due after 1 year	=	Non-current liabilities

What is 'current'?

Under UK GAAP the term 'current assets' has always implied those items that will be realized in the next 12-month period. If debtors are collectible in more than 12 months and yet included within current assets then separate disclosure is required in the notes.

Internationally the terms 'receivable' and 'payable' have a stronger correlation to the operating cycle of the business (i.e. the time period between the acquisition of assets for processing/resale and their realization in cash or cash equivalents) where this exceeds one year. Only if the operating cycle cannot be clearly identified would 12 months be used as the default period.

For non-operating assets and liabilities such as an interest accrual the 12-month cut-off would still be appropriate.

Analytical consequences

For most businesses the consequences for analysis arising from balance-sheet presentation are modest subject to the caveat of greater care being taken until familiar with the new terminology and so on.

For businesses with an unusual length of operating cycle greater care would be needed in making a comparison with a business from a different sector.

Main sources of guidance

UK GAAP

- ◆ Companies Act 1985.

International GAAP

- ◆ IAS 1 *Presentation of Financial Statements.*

Key Facts

1. Key differences in balance-sheet presentation between UK and international GAAP lie in
   - ◆ Terminology
   - ◆ International emphasis on the operating cycle
   - ◆ Formats prescribed by legislation in the UK giving way to a more flexible international approach
   - ◆ Most UK balance sheets have net assets as their total whereas international balance sheets aggregate assets and liabilities/equity separately.

Presentation – The Performance Statement

Setting expectations

Under UK GAAP the dominant performance statement is the profit and loss account. The same is true of international GAAP but this document is now labelled the income statement.

Illustrations

Box 6.1   Halfords plc (2005) – UK GAAP

Group Profit and Loss Account

For the period	Notes	52 weeks to 1 April 2005 £m	53 weeks to 2 April 2004 £m
Turnover	1	**628.4**	578.6
Cost of sales		**(290.7)**	(269.0)
Gross profit		**337.7**	309.6
Net operating expenses	2	**(259.4)**	(244.1)
Operating profit before goodwill amortisation and exceptional operating items		**92.2**	79.2
Goodwill amortisation		**(13.7)**	(13.7)
Exceptional operating items	3	**(0.2)**	–
Operating profit	4	**78.3**	65.5
Profit on disposal of fixed assets	5	–	6.4
Net interest payable, before net exceptional interest income/(charges)		**(14.7)**	(35.4)
Net exceptional interest income/(charges)		**0.5**	(8.7)
Net interest payable	7	**(14.2)**	(44.1)
Profit on ordinary activities before taxation		**64.1**	27.8
Taxation on profit on ordinary activities	8	**(24.2)**	(14.3)

43

Profit on ordinary activities		**39.9**	13.5
after taxation			
Equity dividends	9	**(27.4)**	–
Retained profit for the		**12.5**	13.5
financial period			

Earnings per 1p share			
Basic	11	**18.5p**	8.3p
Diluted	11	**18.5p**	8.0p
Earnings per 1p share			
before goodwill			
amortisation and			
exceptional items			
Basic	11	**24.4p**	17.7p
Diluted	11	**24.4p**	16.9p

i) All results relate to continuing operations of the Group.

ii) There is no material difference between the results as stated above and their historical cost equivalents.

iii) The Group has no recognised gains and losses other than the profits above and therefore no separate Statement of Total Recognised Gains and Losses has been presented

Box 6.2   Halfords plc (2006) – International GAAP

Consolidated Income Statement

For the period

	Notes	52 weeks to 31 March 2006 £m	52 weeks to 1 April 2005 £m
Revenue	1	681.7	628.4
Cost of sales		(335.0)	(292.0)
Gross profit		346.7	336.4
Operating expenses	2	(257.6)	(247.1)
Operating profit	4	89.1	89.3

Finance costs	6	(12.5)	(15.4)
Finance income	6	0.4	0.4
Profit before tax		77.0	74.3
Taxation	7	(23.4)	(23.2)
Profit attributable to equity shareholders		53.6	51.1
Earnings per share Basic	9	23.6p	23.7p

All results relate to continuing operations of the Group.

Key differences

General layout

Schedule 4 Companies Act 1985 specifies four profit and loss account formats.

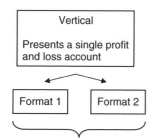
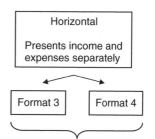

This allows a greater disparity of presentational styles for the profit and loss account than is seen for the UK balance sheet.

Box 6.1 is a Format 1 profit and loss account, but operating expenses have been aggregated rather than analysing separately into distribution and administration costs.

Internationally IAS 1 does not give a prescribed format, but does specify a minimum disclosure that must be given on the face of the income statement.

◆ Revenue
◆ Finance costs
◆ Share of the profit or loss of associates and joint ventures accounted for using the equity method
◆ Tax expense
◆ A single amount comprising (i) the total post-tax profit or loss of discontinued operations and (ii) the post-tax gain or loss recognized on the measurement to fair value less costs to sell or on the disposal of the assets or disposal group(s) constituting the discontinued operation
[Do not be disconcerted by this disclosure we will look at it in more detail later in the chapter]
◆ Profit or loss.

Classification by either nature or function of expense is allowed.

Dealing with the unusual

One of the main requirements of an analyst of financial information is to have sufficient information such that the performance of ongoing activities can be distinguished from one-off events or parts of the business that are subsequently to be discontinued or sold.

Under UK GAAP one-off events can be technically placed into three categories, but one of these is effectively redundant.

1. Extraordinary items – these are items that are material to an understanding of the business and also outside the normal course of business. It is the latter part of this description that renders this term obsolete as there are no events that are readily categorized outside the normal course of business. The bottom line is that you would not expect to see an item designated as extraordinary in a set of accounts prepared under UK GAAP.

2. Super-exceptionals (also known as non-operating exceptional items) – these are material one-off events that, although within the normal course of business, require separate disclosure on the face of the profit and loss account below operating profit. There are three items specified within this category:
   (i) Profits or losses on the sale or termination of an operation
   (ii) Costs of a fundamental reorganization or restructuring having a material effect on the nature and focus of the reporting entities' operations

(iii) Profits or losses on the disposal of fixed assets as seen in Box 6.1.

3. Other operating exceptionals – these can be shown on the face of the profit and loss account or in the notes

International practice now specifically prohibits extraordinary items. It also does not specifically use the term 'exceptional', but does acknowledge that the nature of certain items does warrant separate disclosure. Typical items of this sort would include substantial write-downs in value and litigation settlements.

Care should be taken if reviewing financial statements compliant with international GAAP prior to 2004 as before the IASB's Improvements Project extraordinary items were allowed.

In practice the disclosure of exceptional items can take numerous forms with companies often giving comprehensive disclosure to aid stakeholder understanding (Box 6.3), and the term 'exceptional' remains the most common phrasing.

Discontinued operations

This is a subject that requires particular care as it is vital to understanding the future prospects of a business, and has been an area of substantial change.

Under UK GAAP the main source of guidance is FRS 3 *Reporting Financial Performance* and requires the preparer of the financial statements to consider the answer to two key decisions.

1. Is the activity discontinued?
2. Should a provision be made?

Although these are commercially intertwined from an accounting perspective they must be considered separately.

Is the activity discontinued?

To answer yes to this question all of the following conditions must be met.

◆ The sale or termination is completed either in the period or before the earlier of 3 months after the commencement of the subsequent period and the date on which the financial statements are approved.
◆ Activity has ceased permanently.

Box 6.3 Woolworths Group plc (2006)

Group Income Statement

for the 52 weeks ended 28 January 2006 and 29 January 2005

	Note	52 weeks to 28 January 2006			52 weeks to 29 January 2005		
		Before exceptional items £m	Exceptional items (Note 6) £m	Total £m	Before exceptional items £m	Exceptional items (Note 6) £m	Total £m
Continuing operations							
Revenue	1	2,630.7	–	2,630.7	2,742.4	–	2,742.4
Cost of goods sold		(1,940.7)	6.0	(1,934.7)	(1,996.2)	(17.3)	(2,015.5)
Gross profit		690.0	6.0	696.0	744.2	(17.3)	726.9
Selling and marketing costs		(534.1)	–	(534.1)	(560.2)	–	(560.2)
Administrative expenses		(124.7)	11.8	(112.9)	(134.1)	(43.4)	(177.5)
Other operating income		21.9	–	21.9	16.1	2.9	19.0
Operating profit		53.1	17.8	70.9	66.0	(57.8)	8.2
Interest payable and similar charges	2	(13.7)	–	(13.7)	(14.6)	–	(14.6)
Interest receivable	3	4.3	–	4.3	3.5	–	3.5
Profit/(loss) before taxation	1	43.7	17.8	61.5	54.9	(57.8)	(2.9)
Taxation	8	(13.3)	(6.9)	(20.2)	(19.0)	14.4	(4.6)

	Note						
Profit/(loss) for the year from continuing operations after taxation		30.4	10.9	41.3	35.9	(43.4)	(7.5)
Discontinued operations							
Loss after taxation for the year from discontinued operations	7	(5.1)	(26.0)	(31.1)	(0.6)	–	(0.6)
Profit/(loss) for the year	4	25.3	(15.1)	10.2	35.3	(43.4)	(8.1)
Attributable tax							
Equity shareholders		25.2	(15.1)	10.1	35.1	(43.4)	(8.3)
Minority interest		0.1	–	0.1	0.2	–	0.2
	30	25.3	(15.1)	10.2	35.3	(43.4)	(8.1)
Earnings/(loss) per share (pence)	10						
Basic				0.7			(0.6)
Diluted				0.7			(0.6)
Earnings/(loss) per share from continuing operations (pence)	10						
Basic				2.8			(0.5)
Diluted				2.8			(0.5)

- The sale or termination has a material effect on the focus and nature of the reporting entity's operations.
- The assets, liabilities, results of operations and activities are clearly distinguishable.

Consider the following example.

Example 6.1

Determining discontinued status

ABC plc has historically been involved in the retail of consumer goods, provision of financial services and manufacture on behalf of third parties. The latter had been the primary business of the company when originally incorporated, but now represents only 12% of revenues. It has a financial year end of 31 December, and is preparing the financial statements for 2006.

On 23 February 2005 the board decided to cease manufacturing by the end of the month – the short time scale being to curtail heavy losses accruing within this division.

The directors signed off the 2004 accounts on 3 March 2005.

Would the manufacturing division be presented as a discontinued operation in the 2004 accounts?

Based on the information available this is a discontinued operation.

The division had been discontinued in the 3-month period post the financial year end and before the accounts were approved for release. At 12 per cent of revenues it remains material, and as a loss-making entity there is no suggestion that there is any intention to revive this element of the business at a later date. Finally the nature of manufacture is sufficiently distinct from the other strands of the business that they can be separately identified.

There is no prescribed threshold for materiality in UK or international GAAP, but typical broad brush guidelines used by those that audit financial statements are

- 0.5–1 per cent of revenues
- 1–2 per cent of gross assets
- 5–10 per cent of profits (always take extreme care with this parameter as it can vary enormously from period to period).

The UK GAAP profit and loss account adopts a columnar format showing the user continuing and discontinued operations; and a comprehensive example showing the columnar format and presentation of exceptional items is shown in Box 6.4.

Box 6.4 BT Group plc (2002) – Profit and loss account extract

Group profit and loss account
for the year ended 31 March 2002

| | Notes | Continuing activities | | | Discontinued activities and intra-group items £m | Total £m |
		Before goodwill amortisation and exceptional items £m	Goodwill amortisation and exceptional items £m	Total continuing activities £m		
Total turnover	2	21,815	–	**21,815**	2,827	**24,642**
Group's share of joint ventures' turnover	3	(2,752)	–	**(2,752)**	(76)	**(2,828)**
Group's share of associates' turnover	3	(1,297)	–	**(1,297)**	(639)	**(1,936)**
Trading between group and principal joint venture	3	681	–	**681**	–	**681**
Group turnover	2	18,447	–	**18,447**	2,112	**20,559**
Other operating income	4	361	–	**361**	1	**362**
Operating costs	5	(16,037)	(2,817)	**(18,854)**	(2,546)	**(21,400)**
Group operating profit (loss)		2,771	(2,817)	**(46)**	(433)	**(479)**
Group's share of operating profit (loss) of joint ventures	6	(323)	(1,160)	**(1,483)**	19	**(1,464)**
Group's share of operating profit (loss) of associates	6	215	(175)	**40**	43	**83**
Total operating profit (loss)		2,663	(4,152)	**(1,489)**	(371)	**(1,860)**
Profit on sale of fixed asset investments	7	–	169	**169**	3,208	**3,377**
Profit (loss) on sale of group undertakings	7	–	(148)	**(148)**	1,160	**1,012**
Profit on sale of property fixed assets	8	27	1,062	**1,089**	–	**1,089**
Interest receivable	10	360	–	**360**	–	**360**
Amounts written off investments	9	–	(535)	**(535)**	–	**(535)**
Interest payable	11	(1,777)	(162)	**(1,939)**	(43)	**(1,982)**
Profit (loss) on ordinary activities before taxation		1,273	(3,766)	**(2,493)**	3,954	**1,461**

Non-operating exceptionals

Should a provision be made?

A provision can only be made if it can be shown that the entity is demonstrably committed as would be the case with a binding sale agreement or a public announcement.

The amount of the provision is very contentious as it includes direct costs (e.g. redundancy costs) plus any operating losses up to the date of sale or termination. The latter goes against all other current accounting practice which does not allow the anticipation of future events.

The fact that UK GAAP requires two separate questions to be answered when looking at discontinued activities can also lead to some interesting presentational consequences.

Example 6.2

UK GAAP – The interrelationship between the determination of discontinued operations and the need to provide

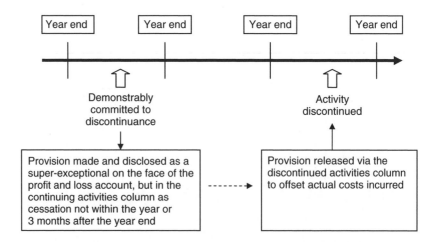

Under international GAAP there have been some significant changes in the approach to discontinued operations since 2004 with the release of IFRS 5 *Non-current Assets Held for Sale and Discontinued Operations* – the first IFRS to result from direct collaboration between IASB and US FASB. This describes a discontinued operation as a component of an entity that either has been disposed of or is classified as held for sale and

◆ represents a separate major line of business or geographical area of operations;

- is part of a single co-ordinated plan to dispose of a separate major line of business or geographical area of operations; or
- is a subsidiary acquired exclusively for resale.

The term 'held for sale' is crucial to designation as discontinued and an asset or disposal group of assets can only be so designated if:

- management is committed to a plan to sell
- available for immediate sale in its present condition
- an active programme to locate a buyer is initiated
- sale must be highly probable within 12 months
- the asset is being genuinely marketed for sale at a sales price reasonable in relation to its fair value
- actions required to complete the plan indicate that it is unlikely the plan will be significantly changed or withdrawn.

Immediately prior to being designated as held for sale the assets involved are valued using the applicable IAS/IFRS. This ensures that any profit or loss arising on being so designated is solely attributable to that change in status rather than ongoing valuation issues that would have been applicable had the assets remained part of the business long term.

53

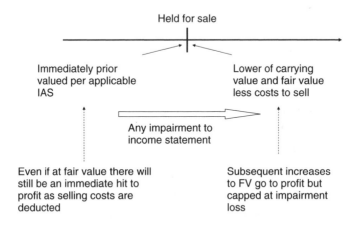

Illustration 6.5 The consequences of being designated as held for sale

It should be clear that there are significant differences in the designation of discontinued activities under UK GAAP and assets held

for sale under international GAAP, but the latter holds two more major differences.

1. At the moment an asset or disposal group is designated as held for sale, all depreciation of non-current assets so classified stops
2. Presentation within the accounts.

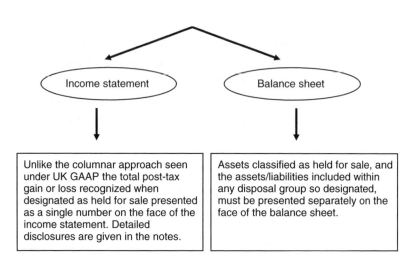

Analytical consequences

The fundamental differences between the UK profit and loss account and the international income statement are modest, particularly as most companies making the transition will try to ensure a familiar presentational style is given to stakeholders.

However there are some significant differences in both the definition and disclosure of one-off items. Particular care is needed when comparing with a copy of the previous year's financial statements as it will not always be true that a UK discontinued operation equates to an international one held for sale operation. It will also be necessary to make more extensive use of the accompanying notes under international GAAP to fully understand the repercussions for the figures.

Box 6.5 J Sainsbury plc (2005) – Income statement extracts

Group income statement
for the 52 weeks to 25 March 2006

	Note	2006 £m	2005 £m
Continuing operations			
Revenue	3	**16,061**	15,202
Cost of sales		**(14,994)**	(14,544)
Gross profit		**1,067**	658
Administrative expenses		**(839)**	(830)
Other income		**1**	21
Operating profit/(loss)	4	**229**	(151)
Finance income	5	**30**	44
Finance costs	5	**(155)**	(132)
Share pf post-tax profit from joint ventures		**–**	1
Profit/(loss) before taxation		**104**	(238)
Analysed as:			
Underlying profit before tax from continuing operations'		**267**	238
Business Review and Transformation operating costs	7	**(51)**	(497)
IT insourcing costs	9	**(63)**	–
Profit on sale of properties	4	**1**	21
Financing fair value movements	5	**(12)**	–
Debt restructuring costs	5	**(38)**	–
		104	(238)
Income tax (expense)/credit	9	**(46)**	51
Profit/(loss) from continuing operations		**58**	(187)
Discontinued operations			
Profit attributable to discontinued operations		**–**	375
Profit for the financial year		**·58**	188
Attributable to:			
Equity holders of the parent		**64**	184
Minority interests		**(6)**	4
		58	188
Earnings/(losses) per share	10	**pence**	pence
Basic		**3.8**	4.1
Diluted		**3.8**	4.1
From continuing operations:			
Basic		**3.8**	(17.4)
Diluted		**3.8**	(17.4)

[1] Profit before tax from continuing operations before any gain or loss on the sale of properties, impairment of goodwill, financing fair value movements and one off items that are materialand infrequent innature. In the current financial year, these one off items were the Business Review costs, IT insourcing costs and debt restructuring costs. In the prior financial year, these one off items were the Business Review and Transformation costs.

Main sources of guidance

UK GAAP

- Companies Act 1985
- FRS 3 *Reporting Financial Performance.*

International GAAP

- IAS 1 *Presentation of Financial Statements*
- IFRS 5 *Non-current Assets Held for Sale and Discontinued Operations.*

Key Facts

1. UK profit and loss formats are largely dictated by statutory formats, but in practice the international income statement will look very familiar.
2. There is no requirement under international GAAP to formally distinguish between super-exceptional and other exceptional items.
3. A discontinued operation under UK GAAP is fundamentally a material and separable operation discontinued within the year or the 3-month period following the year end (assuming the financial statements are not approved earlier).

   Under international GAAP IFRS 5 focuses on operations discontinued within the year or which meet the criteria to be classified as held for sale. Unlike the UK columnar disclosure for discontinued operations international GAAP only requires the post-tax gain or loss to be shown on the face of the income statement. However, many companies will give supplemental disclosure to avoid confusion.
4. When non-current assets are held for sale, depreciation ceases.

Presentation – The Cash Flow Statement

Setting expectations

Understanding the key influences on the cash position of a business and its rate of cash burn are fundamental in determining its prospects of survival. Users of the international cash flow statement will notice some significant changes to the UK equivalent both in terms of its presentation and in the fundamental issue of what the statement is reconciling.

Illustrations

Box 7.1 SABMiller plc (2005) – UK GAAP

Consolidated cash flow statements

for the years ended 31 March

	Notes	**2005 US$m**	2004 US$m
Net cash inflow from operating activities	25	**2,792**	2,292
Dividends received from associates		**47**	25
Returns on investments and servicing of finance			
Interest received		**94**	53
Interest paid		**(228)**	(216)
Interest element of finance lease rental payments		**(2)**	(3)
Dividends received from other investments		**10**	9
Dividends paid to minority interests		**(172)**	(154)
Net cash outflow from returns on investments and servicing of finance		**(298)**	(311)
Taxation paid		**(625)**	(456)
Capital expenditure and financial investments			
Purchase of tangible fixed assets		**(768)**	(576)

Sale of tangible fixed assets		**30**	27
Purchase of investments		**(19)**	(217)
Sale of investments		**475**	6
Net cash outflow for capital expenditure and financial investments		**(282)**	(760)
Acquisitions and disposals			
Purchase of subsidiary undertakings	29	**(24)**	(338)
Net cash/(overdraft) acquired with subsidiary undertakings	29	**1**	(160)
Purchase of shares from minorities	29	**(793)**	(20)
Purchase of shares in associates		**(13)**	(58)
Net funding (to)/from associates		**(68)**	1
Proceeds of pension fund surplus from previously disposed operation	5	**–**	47
Proceeds from disposal of trademarks	5	**–**	13
Net cash outflow for acquisitions and disposals		**(897)**	(515)
Equity dividends paid to shareholders		**(412)**	(309)
Management of liquid resources			
Sale/(purchase) of short-term liquid instruments		**3**	(16)
Cash placed in short-term deposits		**(661)**	–
Net cash outflow from management of liquid resources	26, 27	**(658)**	(16)
Financing			
Issue of shares		**38**	10
Issue of shares to minorities		**1**	4
Net purchase of own shares for share trusts		**(21)**	(10)
New loans raised	26, 27	**540**	3,385
Repayment of loans	26, 27	**(658)**	(3,377)
Net cash (outflow)/inflow from financing		**(100)**	12
Decrease in cash in the year	26, 27	**(433)**	(38)

Box 7.2   SABMiller plc (2006) – International GAAP

Consolidated cash flow statements

for the years ended 31 March

	Notes	**2006** **US$m**	2005 US$m
Cash flows from operating activities			
Net cash generated from operations	25a	**3,291**	2,792
Interest received		**80**	94
Interest paid		**(401)**	(228)
Interest element of finance lease rental payments		**–**	(2)
Tax paid		**(869)**	(625)
Net cash from operating activities		**2,101**	2,031
Cash flows from investing activities			
Purchase of property, plant and equipment		**(999)**	(756)
Proceeds from sale of property, plant and equipment		**48**	30
Purchase of intangible assets		**(33)**	(12)
Purchase of investments		**(7)**	(19)
Proceeds from sale of investments		**5**	475
Acquisition of subsidiaries (net of cash acquired)		**(717)**	(23)
Purchase of shares from minorities		**(2,048)**	(793)
Purchase of shares in associates		**(1)**	(13)
Funding to associates		**–**	(68)
Repayment of funding by associates		**122**	–
Dividends received from associates		**71**	47
Dividends received from other investments		**2**	10
Net cash used in investing activities		**(3,557)**	(1,122)
Cash flows from financing activities			
Proceeds from the issue of shares		**30**	38

Proceeds from the issue of shares to minorities		–	1
Purchase of own shares for share trusts		**(8)**	(21)
Proceeds from borrowings	25b	**3,002**	540
Repayment of borrowings	25b	**(900)**	(632)
Capital element of finance lease payments	25b	**(28)**	(25)
Increase in loan participation deposit	25b	**(196)**	–
Dividends paid to shareholders of the parent		**(520)**	(412)
Dividends paid to minority interests		**(167)**	(172)
Net cash generated/(used) in financing activities		**1,213**	(683)
Net cash from operating, investing and financing activities		**(243)**	226
Effects of exchange rate changes		11	(56)
Net (decrease)/increase in cash and cash equivalents	25b	**(232)**	170
Cash and cash equivalents at 1 April	25b	**630**	460
Cash and cash equivalents at 31 March	25b	**398**	630

What is cash?

The fact that accounts prepared under UK or international GAAP refer to this statement as a cash flow could lead to the supposition that they are identical – sadly this is not true!

The UK cash flow statement shows all the movements that reconcile the opening and closing 'pure' cash positions. Cash in this context comprises cash-in-hand plus deposits repayable on demand-less overdrafts.

The international cash flow statement reconciles cash and cash equivalents. The latter comprise short-term highly liquid investments that are readily convertible into known amounts of cash. They typically have less than 3 months to maturity when acquired with short-dated government stock being a good example. Within the UK format these would represent one of the movements on the cash flow and be included within the liquid resources section of the proforma.

Cash flow classification

The UK layout has numerous headings that act as pigeon holes for the cash flows that they represent, and also provides some clues to the identification of free cash. Many financial institutions have their own definition of free cash, but in broad terms this is the cash available to a business to use at it own discretion after obligatory cash payments have been made. Consider the headings of the UK cash flow statement:

- Cash flows from operating activities
- Dividends from joint ventures and associates
- Returns on investment and servicing of finance
- Taxation
- Capital expenditure and financial investment
- Acquisitions and disposals
- Equity dividends paid
- Management of liquid resources
- Financing.

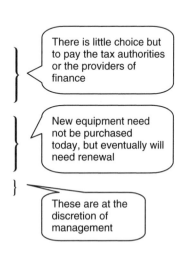

There is little choice but to pay the tax authorities or the providers of finance

New equipment need not be purchased today, but eventually will need renewal

These are at the discretion of management

The international cash flow statement has just three sections and these reflect the same structure as used for US cash flow reporting.

Table 7.1 Classification of cash flows

UK GAAP	International GAAP
Net cash flow from operating activities	Operating
Dividends from joint ventures and associates	Discretionary but must be consistent
Returns on investment and servicing of finance	Discretionary but must be consistent
Taxation	Discretionary but must be consistent
Capital expenditure and financial investment	Investing
Acquisitions and disposals	Investing
Equity dividends paid	Discretionary but must be consistent
Management of liquid resources	Effectively now part of the opening and closing position to be reconciled. Otherwise within financing if the definition of a cash equivalent is not met
Financing	Financing

As with other international formats there is some flexibility in the allocation to each heading providing that the company is consistent year on year. Table 7.1 shows how to map a cash flow between the two formats.

Is a cash flow statement always required?

The simple answer to this question under international GAAP is yes, but under UK GAAP there are a number of exemptions, the most noteworthy being that companies qualifying as small are exempt from the requirement to produce a cash flow statement.

Treasury management

Large businesses are not funded exclusively with cash, and often have a complex treasury management function that controls over-all funding and does not focus exclusively on operations. This is directly reflected under UK GAAP via a requirement to provide both an analysis and reconciliation of net debt (i.e. debt-less cash and liquid resources).

Box 7.3 SABMiller plc (2005) – Reconciliation of net cash flow to movement in net debt

26. Reconciliation of net cash flow to movement in net debt

	2005 US$m	2004 US$m
Decrease in cash	**(433)**	(38)
Net cash outflow/(inflow) from decrease/(increase) in debt and lease financing	**118**	(8)
Net cash outflow from increase in liquid resources	**658**	16
Change in net debt resulting from cash flows	**343**	(30)
Loans and finance leases acquired with subsidiary undertakings	–	(82)
Loans and finance leases reclassified to fixed asset investments	–	9
Exchange movements	**(104)**	(7)
Amortisation of bond costs	**(7)**	(9)
Conversion of debt	**597**	–
Cash inflow from interest rate hedges	–	56
Movement in net debt in the year	**829**	(63)
Opening net debt	**(3,025)**	(2,962)
Closing net debt	**(2,196)**	(3,025)

A total of US$56 million was received in 2004 in relation to the interest rate hedges on the bonds issued in the year: which is being amortised through the profit and loss account over the life of the bonds.

Box 7.4 SABMiller plc (2005) – Analysis of net debt (extract)

27. Analysis of net debt

	Cash at bank and in hand	Overdraft	Total	Funding due within one year	Funding due after one year	Finance leases due within one year	Finance leases due after one year	Total	Liquid resources	Net debt
	US$m	US$m	US$m	US$m	US$m	US$m	US$m	US$m	US$m	US$m
At 31 March 2003	559	(118)	441	(2,271)	(1,084)	(20)	(30)	(3,405)	2	(2,962)
Cash flow	58	(96)	(38)	2,030	(2,055)	22	(5)	(8)	16	(30)
Acquisitions (excluding cash and overdrafts)	–	–	–	(1)	(95)	–	–	(96)	14	(62)
Reclassifications	–	–	–	8	2	–	–	10	(1)	9
Exchange adjustments	34	(8)	26	(17)	(7)	(4)	(5)	(33)	–	(7)
Change in maturity of net debt	–	–	–	(116)	116	(22)	22	–	–	–
Cash inflow from interest rate hedges	–	–	–	–	56	–	–	56	–	56
Amortisation of bond costs	–	–	–	–	(9)	–	–	(9)	–	(9)

At 31 March 2004	651	(222)	429	(367)	(3,076)	(24)	(18)	(3,485)	31	(3,025)
Cash flow	(165)	(268)	(433)	278	(185)	26	(1)	118	658	343
Exchange adjustments	(32)	(24)	(56)	(18)	(29)	(1)	–	(48)	–	(104)
Change in maturity of net debt	–	–	–	(175)	175	(17)	17	–	–	–
Reclassifications	–	1	1	–	–	(1)	–	(1)	–	–
Amortisation of bond costs	–	–	–	(1)	(6)	–	–	(7)	–	(7)
Conversion of debt	–	–	–	–	597	–	–	597	–	597
At 31 March 2005	**454**	**(513)**	**(59)**	**(283)**	**(2,524)**	**(17)**	**(2)**	**(2,826)**	**689**	**(2,196)**

Note: Liquid resources comprises short-term deposits with banks, which mature within 12 months of the date of inception, and amounts invested in short-dated liquid instruments.

Under international GAAP this very specific requirement for net debt disclosures is missing, but many companies will continue to provide at least some elements of this disclosure because of its value to analysts of the financial statements. Additionally new disclosures now required under financial instrument accounting guidance also provide some complementary information.

The international accounting standard on cash flow statements does specifically require an entity to provide such additional disclosures as are needed for a full understanding of the financial position and liquidity. A management commentary is seen as desirable together with information such as:

◆ The amount of undrawn borrowing facilities.
◆ The aggregate amounts of cash flows from each of the operating, investing and financing activities related to interests in joint ventures reported using proportionate consolidation (this is a methodology we will explore further when looking at recommended practice for group accounting).
◆ The aggregate amount of cash flows that represent increases in operating capacity separately from those cash flows that are required to maintain operating capacity.
◆ The amount of cash flows arising from the operating, investing and financing activities of each report industry and geographical segment.

Main sources of guidance
UK GAAP
◆ FRS 1 *Cash Flow Statements*

International GAAP
◆ IAS 7 *Cash Flow Statements*

Key Facts
1. Cash flow statements prepared under UK GAAP reconcile 'pure' cash whereas the international equivalent reconciles cash and cash equivalents.

2. The international cash flow has been simplified to three sections (operating, investing and financing), and there is considerable flexibility as to which sections cash flows are allocated providing there is year-on-year consistency.
3. Under international GAAP there are no exemptions from the requirement to prepare a cash flow statement as an integral part of the accounts.
4. The net debt disclosures provided to clarify treasury management under UK GAAP are not a formal requirement of the international accounting standard, but it does require such additional disclosures as are needed for an understanding of the financial position and liquidity of the entity.

Presentation – Other
Primary Statements and
Associated Disclosures

Setting expectations

In a perfect world every aspect of the performance of a business would be reflected in a single performance statement, and consequentially this would reconcile the opening and closing balance sheets. This is often referred to as the 'all inclusive concept' and remains a goal of the accounting community. However, the production of such a statement requires some significant changes to a wide range of legislation and accounting guidance already in existence, and hence financial statements include supplementary statements that allow users to view all significant activities in the accounting period, and these effectively complement what most non-accountants view as the cornerstones of the accounts, namely

- Balance sheet
- Profit and loss account/income statement
- Cash flow statement.

When these additional statements are considered a prerequisite to the accounts giving a true and fair view they are said to be a primary statement.

Under UK GAAP there is one additional primary statement known as The Statement of Total Recognized Gains and Losses, but it is complemented by additional disclosures that many view as of equal significance.

International GAAP also has one additional primary statement known as The Statement of Changes in Equity which serves a similar purpose. However, companies are allowed an alternative disclosure statement known as a Statement of Recognized Income and Expense which excludes transactions with equity holders. It is not permissible to include both of these statements in the same published accounts.

The UK disclosure requirements derive from FRS 3 *Reporting Financial Performance* which also addresses the issue of non-comparability of financial statements when one entity elects to revalue its tangible fixed assets and another retains them at depreciated historic cost. The disclosure produced is referred to as the 'historic costs note'.

Illustrations

Box 8.1   Tesco plc (2004) – UK GAAP

STATEMENT OF TOTAL RECOGNISED GAINS AND LOSSES

53 weeks ended 28 February 2004

	Group		Company	
	2004 £m	2003 £m	2004 £m	2003 £m
Profit for the financial year	1,100	946	771	618
(Loss)/gain on foreign currency net investments	(157)	22	(2)	–
Total recognised gains and losses relating to the financial year	943	968	769	618

RECONCILIATION OF MOVEMENTS IN SHAREHOLDERS' FUNDS

53 weeks ended 28 February 2004

	Group		Company	
	2004 £m	2003 £m	2004 £m	2003 £m
Profit for the financial year	1,100	946	771	618
Dividends	(516)	(443)	(516)	(443)
	584	503	255	175
(Loss)/gain on foreign currency net investments	(157)	22	(2)	–
New share capital subscribed less expenses	844	421	869	433
Payment of dividends by shares in lieu of cash	158	40	158	40

Net addition to shareholders' funds	1,429	986	1,280	648
Opening shareholders' funds	6,516	5,530	3,257	2,609
Closing shareholders' funds	7,945	6,516	4,537	3,257

Box 8.2 Tesco plc (2006) – International GAAP

Group statement of recognised income and expense Year ended 25 February 2006*

	notes	2006 £m	2005 £m
Gains on revaluation of available-for-sale investments	14	2	–
Foreign currency translation differences		25	11
Actuarial losses on defined benefit pension schemes	23	(442)	(230)
Gains/(losses) on cash flow hedges:			
– net fair value gains		44	–
– reclassified and reported in the Income Statement		(5)	–
Tax on items taken directly to equity	Ö	133	92
Net expense recognised directly in equity		(243)	(127)
Profit for the period		1,576	1,347

Total recognised income and expense for the period	1,333	1,220
Attributable to:		
Equityholders of the parent	1,327	1,217
Minority interests	6	3
	1,333	1,220
Effect of changes in accounting policy (adoption of IAS 32 and IAS 39):	33	
Equityholders of the parent	(314)	
Minority interests	–	
	(314)	

A closer look at UK GAAP

To understand the differences that arise from the transition to international GAAP it is important to examine the UK GAAP disclosures in more detail.

Box 8.3 MC Bridge plc (2005) – Understanding UK
GAAP on reporting performance

Consolidated profit and loss account
for the year ended 30 June 2005

	Note	Pre exceptional items 2005 £m	Exceptional items (note 3) 2005 £m	Post exceptional items 2005 £m
Turnover				
Group and share of joint venture		539.5	–	539.5
Less: share of joint venture's turnover		(2.4)	–	(2.4)
Group turnover	2	537.1	–	537.1
Cost of sales		(348.4)	–	(348.4)
Gross profit		188.7	–	188.7
Distribution costs		(34.0)	–	(34.0)
Administrative costs				
Before goodwill amortisation		(119.7)	(3.0)	(122.7)
Goodwill amortisation		(0.9)	–	(0.9)
Administrative costs including goodwill amortisation		(120.6)	(3.0)	(123.6)
Group operating profit	2	34.1	(3.0)	31.1
Share of joint venture's operating profit		0.1	–	0.1
Total operating profit: Group and share of joint venture		34.2	(3.0)	31.2
Group interest receivable	6	1.4	–	1.4
Group interest payable and similar charges	6	(2.7)	–	(2.7)
Share of joint venture's interest payable and similar charges		(0.1)	–	(0.1)
Profit on ordinary activities before taxation	7	32.8	(3.0)	29.8
Group tax on profit on ordinary activities	8	(10.1)	0.9	(9.2)
Profit on ordinary activities after taxation		22.7	(2.1)	20.6
Equity minority interest		(0.1)	–	(0.1)
Profit for the year		22.6	(2.1)	20.5
Dividends paid and proposed	9	(8.5)	–	(8.5)
Retained profit for the year		14.1	(2.1)	12.0

> The profit after tax but before dividend appropriations acts as the start point for both the statement of total recognized gains and losses and the reconciliation of shareholers funds, thereby linking them together.

Consolidated statement of total recognised gains and losses for the year ended 30 June 2005	2005 £m
Profit for the financial year	20.5
Unrealised foreign currency differences	(0.2)
Total recognised gains and losses for the financial year	20.3

Reconciliation of movements in consolidated shareholders' funds for the year ended 30 June 2005	Note	2005 £m
Profit for the financial year		20.5
Equity dividends		(8.5)
Retained profit		12.0
Ordinary shares repurchased less issued–share capital	19	(0.1)
Ordinary shares repurchased less issued–reserves	21	(6.3)
Unrealised foreign currency differences		(0.2)
Opening equity shareholders' funds		91.7
Closing shareholders' funds		97.1

Further comments

The statement of total recognized gains and losses highlights aspects of performance that have not been reflected in the profit and loss account. The most common entries are

◆ Unrealized surpluses or deficits on the revaluation of properties and any related tax effect
◆ Certain currency translation differences
◆ Prior period adjustments.

The reconciliation of shareholders' funds in effect accomplishes the all-inclusive concept by summarizing all movements in the period which reconcile opening net assets to closing net assets.

The Reconciliation of Shareholders' Funds

	£
Profit for the financial year before dividends	X
Dividends	(X)
	___
	X
Other recognized gains and losses (this is a single figure representing all the movements from the statement of total recognized gains and losses excluding any prior period adjustments)	X/(X)
	___
	X
Other movements such as contributions from shareholders	X
	___
	X
Opening shareholder funds adjusted for any prior period adjustments reflected on the statement of total recognized gains and losses	X
	___
Closing shareholder funds	X

Key differences

The statement of total recognized gains and losses and the reconciliation of shareholders' funds do not exist under international GAAP.

However, they are replaced by the statement of changes in equity which serves a broadly similar purpose. Sadly the latter has no prescribed format although certain minimum disclosures must appear on the face and not in the notes – including the net profit or loss for the period and the cumulative effect of changes in accounting policy and the correction of fundamental errors.

Changes in accounting policy are one of two events, the other being the correction of a fundamental error, which can create the need for a prior period adjustment under UK GAAP. Unfortunately the definition of what constitutes a change in accounting policy is not identical under the two accounting systems.

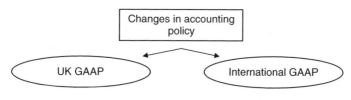

An accounting policy is deemed to have changed if there is a change in the recognition, measurement base or presentation of a transaction. A change does not occur if the only measurement change occurs through the revision of an estimate.

A change of policy occurs if a designated requirement of statute or through to the issue of a new accounting standard. A change also occurs if it can be shown that the relevance and/or reliability of the financial statements has been improved.

The good news is that from a practical perspective the result outcome of the two GAAPs should normally be the same.

The historic costs note

This note is required under UK GAAP by FRS 3 but there is no international equivalent disclosure. Its purpose is to facilitate intercompany comparison when one of the parties has a policy of revaluing tangible long-term assets and the other does not.

When assets are revalued upwards this has two significant potential consequences for the reported performance of a business.

1. The annual depreciation charge will be increased with a consequential reduction in profit.
2. If a revalued asset is sold the profit recognized on disposal will be smaller than for an equivalent asset carried at depreciated

historic cost because some of the increase in value will already have been recognized in assets and equity brought forward from earlier periods.

Box 8.4   Somerfield plc (2005) – Historic costs note

NOTE OF HISTORICAL COST PROFITS AND LOSSES

For the 53 weeks ended 30 April 2005

	2004/2005 (53 weeks) £m	Restated 2003/2004 (52 weeks) £m
Reported profit on ordinary activities before taxation	**60.9**	45.2
Realisation of property revaluation gains of previous years	**10.6**	1.3
Difference between a historical cost depreciation charge and the actual depreciation charge		
for the year calculated on the revalued amount	**2.1**	2.2
Historical cost profit on ordinary activities before taxation	**73.6**	48.7
Historical cost profit for the year retained after taxation and dividends	**60.4**	39.8

Main sources of guidance

UK GAAP

♦ FRS 3 *Reporting Financial Performance*
♦ FRS 18 *Accounting Policies.*

International GAAP

♦ IAS 1 *Presentation of Financial Statements*
♦ IAS 8 *Net Profit or Loss for the Period, Fundamental Errors and Changes in Accounting Policies.*

Key Facts

1. The statement of total recognized gains and losses and the reconciliation of shareholders' funds seen under UK GAAP have no direct international GAAP equivalent, but IAS 1 does require the presentation of a statement of changes in equity which achieves a similar purpose.
2. The statement of changes in equity has no stipulated format and so considerable variety will be seen between companies.
3. Only UK GAAP requires a historic cost note which is a useful tool when making inter-company comparisons.
4. The description of what constitutes a change in accounting policy is different between UK and international GAAP, but the practical end result will be similar in most instances.

Presentation – Related Parties and Segmental Disclosures

Setting expectations

When looking in detail at accounting rules and conventions there is a danger of being drawn into the technical detail and losing sight of the fact that financial statements are supposed to assist a user of financial statements and not 'blind them with science'.

Remember that the companies within the EU that must apply IFRS are listed companies preparing consolidated financial statements. By definition this implies that the entities involved will be large and diverse, and a reader of their financial statements requires more than a global overview but a more detailed analysis of their performance in different markets. This is the purpose of segmental reporting, and it will be noted that IFRS rules and disclosures are more stringent than their UK equivalent.

A further expectation of an investor is that the transactions summarized in financial statements have been conducted at arms length and on fair value terms. If this is not true or the potential exists for divergence in the future it is important that users are made aware of this fact. It does not always imply that such activity is inappropriate, but this is a decision that can only be made if such information is openly available. Related party disclosures have been instigated to serve this purpose.

Related party definitions

The international definition of a related party is centred on the ability of one party to control or exercise influence over the operating and financial decisions of another. This includes:

◆ Enterprises controlling, controlled by, or under common control with the reporting enterprise
◆ Associates
◆ Individuals who directly or indirectly own an interest in the voting power of an entity sufficient to exercise influence – this rule extends to the close family members of such an individual
◆ Key management personnel
◆ Enterprises in which a substantial interest in the voting power is owned, directly or indirectly, by the individuals or key management referred to above.

Under UK GAAP the definitions look broadly similar but caution is needed. Let us examine the UK definition and match as appropriate to its IAS counterpart.

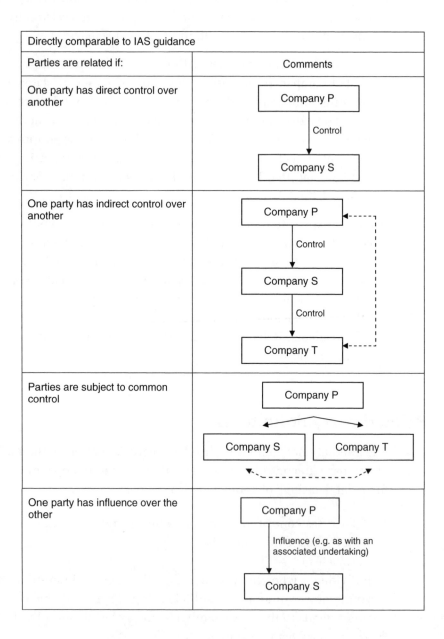

Directly comparable to IAS guidance	
Parties are related if:	Comments
One party has direct control over another	
One party has indirect control over another	
Parties are subject to common control	
One party has influence over the other	

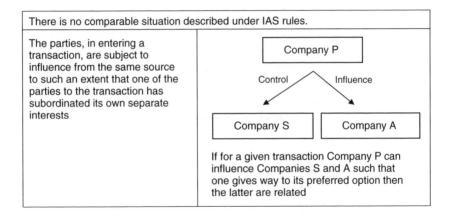

There is no comparable situation described under IAS rules.	
The parties, in entering a transaction, are subject to influence from the same source to such an extent that one of the parties to the transaction has subordinated its own separate interests	Company P Control / Influence Company S Company A If for a given transaction Company P can influence Companies S and A such that one gives way to its preferred option then the latter are related

FRS 8 contains listings of deemed and presumed related parties that is more comprehensive than that described by IAS requirements, and hence there is a possibility of an entity or individual qualifying as a related party under the former and yet escaping the disclosures under international rules.

Materiality

There is a basic premise common to both GAAPs that transactions only need to be disclosed if they are material. However, UK GAAP also contains the concept of two-way materiality when one of the related parties is an individual.

Example 9.1

Materiality of related party transactions under UK GAAP

Companies A, B and C each have annual profits of £100 million. During the course of the last financial year they entered into transactions with a board director.

Under UK GAAP the director is a deemed related party, but the company finance directors now have to consider if the value of the transactions between the parties during the course of the last financial year warrant disclosure.

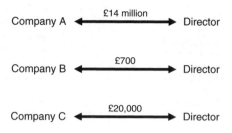

Company A ⟵ £14 million ⟶ Director

Company B ⟵ £700 ⟶ Director

Company C ⟵ £20,000 ⟶ Director

In the case of Company A there is no doubt that the amount is a material-related party transaction as it is material to the company and the individual.

The situation for Company B would seem equally clear-cut as £700 is not material to the company, and is unlikely to be material to a main board director of a public company.

Company C faces more of a dilemma as the amount is not material to the company but may be material to the director. If this is true UK GAAP will require disclosure in the financial statements as it requires a two-way view of materiality when one of the parties to the transaction is an individual.

In practice the situation is made more complex as the normal rules of materiality do not apply when the transaction in question is known to be of disproportionate significance to the users of the accounts – there will always be undue interest in subjects such as director remuneration.

There is no direct equivalent to this two-way view of materiality under IAS. Most companies would recognize that disclosure is still warranted, but the existence of differing guidance always gives scope for interpretation and potential creative accounting.

Related party disclosures

The disclosure requirements of international GAAP are less demanding than the UK equivalent, and it is noteworthy that the former does not specifically require the identification of the related party. However, in practice this information will often be required if users of the financial statements are to understand the significance of the relationship (Box 9.1).

Box 9.1 JJB Sports plc (2006) – International GAAP-related party disclosures

Notes to the Financial statements (continued)

For the 52 weeks to 29 January 2006

41. Related party transactions

During the 52 weeks to 29 January 2006, the Group and Company entered into the following transactions with related parties who are not members of the Group:

	Income		Expenditure	
	52 weeks to 29 January 2006 £'000	53 weeks to 30 January 2005 £'000	52 weeks to 29 January 2006 £'000	53 weeks to 30 January 2005 £'000
Whelco Holdings Limited	163	134	968	778
Executive Director's family trust	–	83	150	150

	Amounts owed by Related Parties		Amounts owed to Related Parties	
	At 29 January 2006 £'000	At 30 January 2005 £'000	At 29 January 2006 £'000	At 30 January 2005 £'000
Whelco Holdings Limited	101	76	24	81

Whelco Holdings Limited is a company owned by members of the family of an Executive Director of JJB, operating itself or through its subsidiaries a number of businesses including that of Wigan Athletic Football Club (WAFC), Wigan Warriors Rugby League Club (WWRLC) and the stadium in which both teams play which is known as the "JJB Stadium".

JJB incurred expenditure in its capacity of sponsors to WAFC and WWRLC and incurred costs in respect of the naming rights for the

JJB Stadium. Advice was taken from independent third parties as to the comparative levels of the costs of sponsorship and naming rights at other clubs and stadia, prior to the agreement of the amounts to be paid.

The Group has made sales to Whelco Holdings limited and its subsidiary companies in respect of both football and rugby related products.

A store in Northampton had previously been leased by JJB from a third party for a number of years and at which it had operated a retail store until October 1998. The freehold of the store was subsequently acquired from the third party by the Trustees of an Executive Director's Accumulation and Maintenance Settlement (a Settlement in which some members of the family of one of JJB's Executive Directors has an interest). JJB initially paid for certain development costs of the site, with the Settlement subsequently reimbursing JJB in full in January 2005, inclusive of interest charges on the debt, which were charged at 1 per cent above base rate. Following the opening of the new retail store on 10 August 2003, JJB has continued to pay rent on a full commercial basis at the rate of £150,000 per annum.

The scope of segmental reporting

There would be little dispute that segmental reporting is most relevant for large companies with diverse operations and a large stakeholder base. This is reflected in UK and international GAAP, but the two are not identical.

UK GAAP	IAS
Public companies	Entities with equity or debt that is publicly traded
Companies that have a listed subsidiary banking and insurance companies, or groups	Entities that are in the process of issuing equity or debt securities in public securities markets
Companies which exceed the medium-sized companies' criteria by a factor of more than 10	Other entities that voluntarily disclose segmental information

The UK requirement to look at a multiple of size criteria set by company law is the most unusual with no direct international equivalent. At 1 January 2007 the medium company size limits are

◆ Turnover not more than
  £22.8 million
◆ Gross assets not more than
  £11.4 million
◆ Not more than 250
  employees

At 10 times these limits the segmental reporting rules of the UK are focussed on substantial entities

UK GAAP has one further idiosyncrasy in the form of the seriously prejudicial rule. This allows a company to omit segmental disclosures if it believes them to be seriously prejudicial to the interests of the business. Circumstances when this might be invoked would be for a company that identified that it was the only one within its sector required to give the disclosures and hence would be providing information to its competitors that would not be reciprocated. International accounting rules do not allow avoidance of segmental disclosures on the grounds of it being seriously prejudicial.

What is a segment?

Both accounting regimes require segmental analysis in terms of business type and geographical spread, but the conceptual basis for determining a segment and the quantitative measures which determine if disclosure is required differ considerably.

UK GAAP leaves the determination of what constitutes a segment to the discretion of the directors, although it does provide some guidelines.

IAS 14 Segment reporting uses a 'management approach' which requires consistency between the segments used for internal reporting.

Following the segment identification a company must determine which of these require disclosure, and it is in this context that the rules again differ markedly.

UK GAAP designates a segment as requiring separate disclosure if it represents 10 per cent or more of:

◆ third party turnover; or
◆ net assets; or
◆ the total of segments in profit or the total of segments in loss (whichever is the greater).

Example 9.2 demonstrates how the last of these tests would apply.

Example 9.2

Identifying reportable segments (UK GAAP)

The management team of XYZ plc have identified eight segments within the company, but are now trying to determine which of these require to be separately reported based on their results. They are particularly nervous regarding segment G and have asked for your assistance.

Segment	Profit £m	Loss £m
A	100	
B	–	40
C	85	–
D	–	80
E	15	–
F	–	65
G	25	–
H	–	70
	225	**255**

The total of loss-making segments is greater than those in profit and hence this will be used as our benchmark; it does not matter that segment G is making a profit.

The key question is: Is 25 > 10% (255)?

The answer is no and hence based on this criteria XYZ plc is not required to report segment G separately.

The international rules for determining a reportable segment are more complex, and require a systematic approach.

Step 1

For each segment determine if the majority of its sales are external and not to other group members.

If the majority of sales are external then proceed to step 2, but if not then the process stops and the segment is not reportable.

> NOTE: If a segment 'fails' in step 1 but its sales to external customers are 10% or more of total external sales, some additional disclosures are required.

Step 2

This applies a similar 10 per cent rule to that seen under UK GAAP, but take care as the subject matter is subtlety different.

Does the segment represent 10 per cent or more of:

- ◆ total segment revenue (internal and external)
- ◆ segment result (again looking at the total of segments in profit and total of segments in loss)
- ◆ total assets.

If the answer is yes then the segment must be separately reported.

Step 3

Check to ensure that the total external revenue attributable to the reportable segments identified by step 2 represent at least 75 per cent of total external revenues.

If the total is below 75 per cent add additional segments, although they failed the 10 per cent test, until the 75 per cent threshold is reached.

Example 9.3

Determining reportable segments under international GAAP

Segment plc, a quoted company, has five different business units reported to the Board in the monthly management accounts. For the most recent year ended 31 December the sales of these five, as a percentage of total sales (internal and external), were as follows:

Business Unit	Internal %	External %	Total %
A	0	38	38
B	0	25	25
C	13	7	20
D	0	9	9
E	0	8	8
	13	**87**	**100**

Which of these units would be classed as reportable under international accounting rules?

The reportable segments are:

Unit A	Has no internal sales and its sales exceed 10% of the total sales of the company
Unit B	As for Unit A
Unit D	Falls below the 10% threshold but is required to reach the 75% of the external sales requirement. [(38+25+9)/87 = 82.7%]

Unit C is not reportable as the majority of its sales are internal.

Segmental disclosures

The core disclosures under UK GAAP are

◆ turnover
◆ result (profit before tax and minority interests)
◆ net assets.

These enable an analyst to calculate returns for each segment and make more informed decisions about the use of funding.

Other disclosures include a distinction between turnover derived from external customers and turnover derived from other segments, and for geographical segments a split of turnover by origin and destination.

In comparison international segmental disclosures are more comprehensive, and require a distinction to be made between business and geographical segments as to which is designated the primary reporting format. Key disclosures for the primary and secondary reporting formats not specifically required by UK GAAP include:

	PRIMARY	SECONDARY
Revenue – Internal	✓	
Revenue – External	✓	✓
Results	✓	
Assets	✓	✓
Liabilities	✓	
Investments in non-current assets	✓	✓
Depreciation/Amortization	✓	

There are further detailed disclosures required, but suffice to say that the disclosures under international GAAP should provide a user with significantly more segmental information than they encountered previously under UK GAAP.

Illustrations of segmental reporting

Box 9.2 Rentokil Initial plc (2004) – Segmental analysis (UK GAAP)

	TURNOVER		PROFIT			
	2004	2003	2004 Profit before exceptional items	2004 Exceptional items (note 3)	2004 Profit after exceptional items	2003
	£m	£m	£m	£m	£m	£m
Geographic analysis						
Continuing operations:						
United Kingdom	1,214.9	1,200.8	177.8	(21.9)	155.9	219.5
Continental Europe	819.5	806.3	160.7	(3.7)	157.0	171.1
North America	265.1	284.4	12.5	(22.9)	(10.4)	17.2
Asia Pacific & Africa	135.8	134.7	44.1	(0.9)	43.2	46.4
Total continuing operations	2,435.3	2,426.2	395.1	(49.4)	345.7	456.2
Discontinued operations	15.5	60.0	0.4	–	0.4	(0.7)
	2,450.8	2,486.2	395.5	(49.4)	346.1	455.5
Less:						
Associate (Asia Pacific & Africa)	(18.5)	(18.7)	–	–	–	–
Franchisees (UK)	(110.2)	(101.2)	–	–	–	–

	2,322.1	2,366.3	395.5	(49.4)	346.1	455.5
Loss on disposal of businesses (note 3)	—	—	—	—	—	(11.7)
Interest (note 4)	—	—	(48.3)	—	(48.3)	(47.0)
	2,322.1	2,366.3	347.2	(49.4)	297.8	396.8
[1]Includes associates	18.5	18.7	4.1		4.1	3.6
Business analysis						
Continuing operations:						
Hygiene Services[2]	759.3	758.1	168.7	(3.7)	165.0	202.6
Pest Control	224.2	224.4	76.8	(0.3)	76.5	84.8
Hygiene	983.5	982.5	245.5	(4.0)	241.5	287.4
Security	574.1	584.0	52.2	—	52.2	58.2
Facilities Management Services[2]	453.8	452.7	28.9	(9.3)	19.6	35.6
Tropical Plants	105.1	112.6	11.9	(10.4)	1.5	17.8
Conferencing	91.1	85.8	25.3	—	25.3	26.4
Facilities Management	650.0	651.1	66.1	(19.7)	46.4	79.8
Parcels Delivery	227.7	208.6	31.3	—	31.3	30.8
Central exceptional items (note 3)	—	—	—	(25.7)	(25.7)	—

Total continuing operations	2,435.3	2,426.2	395.1	(49.4)	345.7	456.2
Discontinued operations	15.5	60.0	0.4	—	0.4	(0.7)
	2,450.8	2,486.2	395.5	(49.4)	346.1	455.5
Less:						
Associate (Hygiene)	(18.5)	(18.7)	—	—	—	—
Franchisees (Parcels Delivery)	(110.2)	(101.2)	—	—	—	—
	2,322.1	2,366.3	395.5	(49.4)	346.1	455.5
Loss on disposal of businesses (note 3)	—	—	—	—	—	(11.7)
Interest (note 4)	—	—	(46.3)	—	(48.3)	(47.0)
	2,322.1	2,366.3	347.2	(49.4)	297.8	396.8
[2] Includes associates						
Hygiene Services	18.5	18.7	3.5	—	3.5	3.2
Facilities Management Services	—	—	0.6	—	0.6	0.4

Box 9.3 Rentokil Initial plc (2005) – Segmental analysis (IAS)

1. Segment Information

(a) Primary reporting format – business segments

At 31 December 2005, the group is organised on a worldwide basis into six main business segments: Textiles and Washroom Services, Pest Control, Tropical Plants, Electronic Security, City Link (represents activities previously categorised as Parcels Delivery) and Facilities Services. There are immaterial sales between the business segments. The segment results for the years ended 31 December 2005 and 31 December 2004 are shown below:

	Revenue		Operating profit	
	2005 £m	2004 £m	2005 £m	2004 £m
Continuing operations				
Textiles and Washroom Services	705.3	686.2	94.3	145.7
Pest Control	246.9	237.5	73.9	78.8
Tropical Plants	112.9	105.1	7.2	7.9
Electronic Security	263.4	242.4	32.8	36.4
City Link	125.5	113.4	29.1	30.3
Manned Guarding	365.2	331.6	11.2	11.3
Other Facilities Services	482.0	465.2	40.5	44.5
Facilities Services	847.2	796.8	51.7	55.8
Central items	–	–	(45.7)	(46.4)
	2,301.2	2,181.4	243.3	308.5
Interest payable and similar charges	–	–	(115.0)	(109.0)

Interest receivable	–	–	59.6	55.4
Share of profit of associates (net of tax)				
– Textiles and Washroom Services	–	–	2.2	1.8
Profit before income tax	–	–	190.1	256.7
Income tax expense	–	–	(51.5)	(69.8)
Total for the year from continuing operations	2,301.2	2,181.4	138.6	186.9
Discontinued operations				
Textiles and Washroom Services	1.3	1.4	0.7	0.4
City Link	0.8	6.6	–	0.9
Other Facilities Services[1]	16.3	41.6	(1.5)	(13.3)
Conferencing	82.9	91.1	186.6	17.2
Total for the year from discontinued operations	101.3	140.7	185.8	5.2
Total for the year (including discontinued)	2,402.5	2,322.1	324.4	192.1
[1]includes associates	–	–	–	0.6

Operating profit in 2005 from Conferencing includes a profit on disposal of £170.3m

Other segment items included in the consolidated income statement are as follows:

	Depreciation		Amortisation	
	2005	2004	2005	2004
	£m	£m	£m	£m
Continuing operations				
Textiles and Washroom Services	101.1	100.9	10.3	11.0
Pest Control	11.7	10.8	2.0	1.5
Tropical Plants	9.4	9.1	4.0	3.8
Electronic Security	5.4	4.7	4.0	2.6
City Link	3.9	3.0	–	–
Manned Guarding	1.8	2.2	3.2	3.1
Other Facilities Services	26.5	23.0	2.6	2.8
Facilities Services	28.3	25.2	5.8	5.9
Central items	1.4	1.5	0.5	0.5
Total for the year from continuing operations	161.2	155.2	26.6	25.3
Discontinued operations				
Textiles and Washroom Services	0.7	1.2	–	–
Other Facilities Services	0.3	0.8	–	0.1
Conferencing	6.2	5.8	–	0.3
Total for the year from discontinued operations	7.2	7.8	–	0.4
Total for the year (including discontinued)	168.4	163.0	26.6	25.7

1 (a) Primary reporting format – business segments (continued)

Property, plant and equipment and intangible asset impairment losses of £31.2m and £2.9m respectively and an inventory impairment loss of £1.0m have been recognised in the Textiles and Washroom Services segment (see notes 12, 13 and 18). In 2004, £9.3m of impairment losses were recognised in the Other Facilities Services segment in discontinued operations. Central items represent corporate expenses that are not capable of being allocated to any business or geographic segment.

The consolidated segment assets and liabilities at 31 December 2005 and 31 December 2004 and capital expenditure for the years then ended are as follows:

	Assets 2005 £m	Assets 2004 £m	Liabilities 2005 £m	Liabilities 2004 £m	Capital expenditure 2005 £m	Capital expenditure 2004 £m
Continuing operations						
Textiles and Washroom Services	472.7	510.0	164.4	164.2	128.0	123.3
Pest Control	101.3	98.2	52.2	50.1	16.8	14.5
Tropical Plants	66.6	57.2	19.7	17.4	17.9	14.1
Electronic Security	165.4	127.9	104.5	95.1	38.0	31.6
City Link	36.5	28.2	11.8	11.6	5.5	4.2
Manned Guarding	82.9	67.5	38.3	34.7	10.2	2.9
Other Facilities Services[1]	238.8	208.0	106.3	94.2	31.2	26.5
Facilities Services	321.7	275.5	144.6	128.9	41.4	29.4
Central items	79.5	225.2	381.4	523.3	8.6	3.2
Total from continuing operations	1,243.7	1,322.2	878.6	990.6	256.2	220.3

Discontinued operations

Textiles and Washroom Services	–	0.8	–	–	0.4	1.1
City Link	–	1.0	–	0.3	0.1	0.4
Other Facilities Services¹	–	8.4	–	6.4	0.1	0.6
Conferencing	–	164.7	–	20.9	10.1	11.2
Total from discontinued operations	–	174.9	–	27.6	10.7	13.3
Total (including discontinued)	1,243.7	1,497.1	878.6	1,018.2	266.9	233.6
¹Includes associates						
– Continuing operations	9.2	8.3	–	–	–	–
– Discontinued operations	–	1.2	–	–	–	–

Reconciliation of segment assets/liabilities to total assets/liabilities

	Assets 2005 £m	Assets 2004 £m	Liabilities 2005 £m	Liabilities 2004 £m
Segment assets/liabilities as above	1,243.7	1,497.1	878.6	1,018.2
Deferred tax assets	74.0	74.0	–	–
Cash and cash equivalents	240.3	199.5	–	–
Current tax liabilities	–	–	115.1	138.4
Bank and other short-term borrowings	–	–	108.5	207.5
Bank and other long-term borrowings	–	–	1,072.1	1,147.1
Deferred tax liabilities	–	–	43.3	43.4
Total assets/liabilities	1,558.0	1,770.6	2,217.6	2,554.6

Segment assets consist of primarily property, plant and equipment, investments, intangible assets, inventories and receivables. Segment liabilities primarily consist of payables and provisions for other liabilities and charges. Cash and cash equivalents and bank and other short/long-term borrowings are managed by group treasury and therefore it is not considered appropriate to analyse these by business or geographic segment. Assets and liabilities are allocated to business and geographic segments on a specific basis.

Capital expenditure comprises additions to property, plant and equipment (note 13) and intangible assets (note 12), including additions resulting from acquisitions through business combinations (note 32).

1 (b) Secondary reporting format – geographical segments

The group manages its business segments on a global basis. The operations are located in the five main geographical areas shown in the table below. The United Kingdom is the home country of the parent company.

The Asia Pacific segment comprises operations based mainly in Australia, New Zealand and South East Asia. The North American segment comprises the USA, Canada and Caribbean businesses.

The revenue analysis in the table below is based on the country where the order is received and would not be materially different if based on the country in which the customer (or total assets) is located.

	Revenue 2005 £m	Revenue 2004 £m	Total assets 2005 £m	Total assets 2004 £m	Capital expenditure 2005 £m	Capital expenditure 2004 £m
Continuing operations						
United Kingdom	1,043.1	1,010.2	359.9	350.6	61.8	68.8
Continental Europe	856.8	813.3	619.8	605.8	141.3	121.5
North America	277.9	244.8	110.2	76.9	27.8	12.3
Asia Pacific[1]	89.6	82.3	57.1	48.2	12.5	11.1
Africa	33.8	30.8	17.2	15.5	4.2	3.4
	2,301.2	2,181.4	1,164.2	1,097.0	247.6	217.1
Central items	–	–	79.5	225.2	8.6	3.2
Total from continuing operations	2,301.2	2,181.4	1,243.7	1,322.2	256.2	220.3
Discontinued operations						
United Kingdom	84.3	97.0	–	166.2	10.1	11.3
Continental Europe	2.7	6.2	–	1.2	0.1	0.8
North America	13.5	33.4	–	5.3	0.4	0.8

Asia Pacific[1]	–	–	–	1.2	–	–
Africa	0.8	4.1	–	1.0	0.1	0.4
Total from discontinued operations	101.3	140.7	–	174.9	10.7	13.3
Total (including discontinued)	2,402.5	2,322.1	1,243.7	1,497.1	266.9	233.6
[1]Includes associates						
– Continuing operations	–	–	9.2	8.3	–	–
– Discontinued operations	–	–	–	1.2	–	–

Analysis of revenue by category

	Continuing operations		Discontinuing operations	
	2005 £m	2004 £m	2005 £m	2004 £m
Contract service revenue (including rental income)	1,769.5	1,675.5	16.3	32.0
Non contract service revenue	428.9	402.2	84.9	108.7
Franchise income	54.2	59.2	–	–
Sales of goods	48.6	44.5	0.1	–
	2,301.2	2,181.4	101.3	140.7

1 (c) Reconciliation of statutory segmental analysis to management divisional analysis

As noted in the Operating Review, the group management structure was reorganised with effect from 1 September 2005. This principally resulted in separate Asia Pacific and South Africa (Other) divisions. For statutory purposes, the businesses within these geographic divisions have been reallocated back to the relevant business segment in line with the requirements of IAS 14 "Segmental Reporting". The commentary in the Operating Review reflects this new divisional structure and not the segmental information presented above. In addition, the commentary in the Operating Review is presented at constant exchange rates and before the amortisation of customer lists and exceptional items. The tables that follow reconcile the segmental information presented above to the divisional performance referred to in the Operating Review on pages 8 to 21.

	Statutory basis 2005 £m	Asia Pacific and other 2005 £m	Foreign exchange 2005 £m	Management basis 2005 £m	Management basis 2004 £m
Revenue from continuing operations					
Textiles and Washroom Services	705.3	(62.3)	(3.2)	639.8	628.2
Pest Control	246.9	(37.5)	(1.2)	208.2	203.8
Tropical Plants	112.9	(10.5)	(0.8)	101.6	95.4
Electronic Security	263.4	–	(0.7)	262.7	242.4
City Link	125.5	–	–	125.5	113.4
Manned Guarding	365.2	–	(5.3)	359.9	331.6
Other Facilities Services	482.0	(12.0)	0.5	469.5	454.2
Facilities Services	847.2	(12.0)	(5.8)	829.4	785.8
Asia Pacific	–	89.6	(2.8)	86.8	82.3
Other	–	32.7	(0.6)	32.1	30.1
	2,301.2	–	(15.1)	2,286.1	2,181.4

	Statutory basis 2005 £m	Asia Pacific and Other 2005 £m	Customer lists and exceptional items 2005 £m	Foreign exchange 2005 £m	Management basis 2005 £m	Management basis 2004 £m
Operating profit from continuing operations						
Textiles and Washroom Services	94.3	(21.6)	42.7	(0.7)	114.7	135.7
Pest Control	73.9	(8.2)	1.5	(0.5)	66.7	70.9
Tropical Plants	7.2	(1.8)	4.1	(0.1)	9.4	9.8
Electronic Security	32.6	–	3.0	–	35.8	38.5
City Link	29.1	–	–	–	29.1	30.4
Manned Guarding	11.2	–	3.0	(0.2)	14.0	14.0
Other Facilities Services	40.5	(5.7)	–	–	34.8	39.2
Facilities Services	51.7	(5.7)	3.0	(0.2)	48.8	53.2
Asia Pacific	–	23.3	–	(0.8)	22.5	25.2
Other	–	12.7	–	(0.1)	12.6	12.5
Central items	(45.7)	1.3	10.9	–	(33.5)	(19.8)
	243.3	–	65.2	(2.4)	306.1	356.4

The future

At the end of 2006 the IASB released IFRS 8 *Operating Segments*. This standard arises from IASB collaboration with the US FASB and will replace IAS 14 *Segment Reporting*.

It adopts a similar management approach to that seen under existing US standards.

Main sources of guidance

UK GAAP

- ◆ FRS 8 *Related Party Disclosures*
- ◆ SSAP 25 *Segmental Reporting*.

International GAAP

- ◆ IAS 24 *Related Party Disclosures*
- ◆ IAS 14 *Segment Reporting*.

Key Facts

1. The definition of a related party under UK GAAP is wider than its international counterpart and hence it is possible that a UK-related party might escape the international net.
2. Segmental reporting per IAS 14 requires more extensive disclosures particularly for the primary reporting format.
3. International rules do not allow the avoidance of segmental disclosures on the grounds that it is seriously prejudicial to the business.

Tangible Non-current Assets

Setting expectations

With the exception of a change in name from 'tangible fixed assets' to 'tangible non-current assets' the fundamentals of accounting for these assets is the same – the devil is in the detail.

Depreciation

Both UK GAAP and its international counterpart require tangible assets, with the exception of land, to be depreciated on a systematic basis. Straight-line depreciation remains the most common approach, but accelerated depreciation methodologies are also employed.

Box 10.1 Woolworths Group plc (2006) – Accounting policy extract (International GAAP)

Property, Plant and Equipment

Property, plant and equipment is stated at cost less accumulated depreciation. Cost includes expenditure that is directly attributable to the acquisition of the items. Depreciation of tangible fixed assets is provided where it is necessary to reflect a reduction from book value to estimated residual value over the estimated useful life of the asset to the Group.

Depreciation of property, plant and equipment is calculated by the straight-line method and the annual rates applicable to the principal categories are:

Land and buildings
- Freeholds   —   2 per cent
- Long leaseholds   —   5 per cent
- Short leaseholds   —   over the life of the lease

Fixtures, fittings and equipment
- **Tenant's improvements**   —   shorter of ten years and the remaining life of the lease
- **Fixtures and fittings**   —   between 10 per cent and 15 per cent

---

– Computers and electronic equipment	–	between 20 per cent and 50 per cent
– Motor cars	–	25 per cent
– Commercial vehicles	–	33% per cent

The Group has adopted a policy of not revaluing freehold properties.

The assets' carrying value and useful lives are reviewed and adjusted, if appropriate, at each balance sheet date. An asset's carrying amount is written down immediately to its recoverable amount if the asset's carrying amount is greater than its estimated recoverable amount.

In 2004 the IASB completed a revisions project updating several of its accounting standards already in issue, one of which was IAS 16 *Property, Plant and Equipment*. This removed a number of 'niggling' differences such as UK GAAP's greater emphasis on the separation of major fixed assets into their component parts such that each could be depreciated separately. The international guidance is now consistent with this.

Some confusion remains about the UK's approach to the annuity method of depreciation, whereby the depreciation charge increases over time, but this would be considered for use so rarely that it is not a practical concern.

Revaluation

Unlike US GAAP which prohibits the upward revaluation of tangible assets this is allowed as an option under both UK and international rules which also have other aspects of this accounting treatment in common.

♦ Cherry-picking of assets to revalue is not permitted, but must be applied to all assets within a class or not at all.
♦ When revaluation is adopted it must be applied consistently, and assets must be reviewed to ensure that valuations are not materially inaccurate.

However, there are also some differences in approach.

What value?

IAS 16 *Property, Plant and Equipment* requires revalued assets to be valued at their fair value.

> Fair value = the amount for which an asset could be exchanged between knowledgeable, willing parties in an arm's length transaction.

In practice fair value is usually market value, but if this is not available then depreciated replacement cost should be used.

Example 10.1

Depreciated replacement cost.

On 1 January 2001 a company purchased a property for £200,000 to which it assigned a 20-year useful economic life and a zero residual value.

The company has elected to revalue all properties to market value but the unique nature and location of the property purchased in 2001 means that a market value is not readily ascertainable.

Estimates from local building firms indicate that the current cost of constructing a similar property would be £500,000.

Accounts are being prepared as at 31 December 2006.

Depreciated replacement cost acknowledges that it is inappropriate to use the £500,000 replacement cost as an approximation to fair value of the existing asset because of wear and tear. To create a like-for-like situation the years of use need to be reflected.

$$\text{Depreciated replacement cost} = £500,000 \times \frac{14}{20} = £350,000$$

UK GAAP gives more detail on the valuation to be applied and it is possible for this value to differ from the international interpretation.

♦ Non-specialized properties at existing use value
♦ Specialized properties to be valued using depreciated replacement cost
♦ Other assets to be valued at market value unless unobtainable, and then use depreciated replacement cost.

> If existing use value and market value differ significantly the latter must be disclosed.
>
> This could occur on a site that would have a significantly higher value if sold for redevelopment.

Frequency of valuation

It is important under any regime allowing revaluation that values are kept updated, but that this does not become too onerous.

UK guidance is more specific on frequency although the reality should be comparable to international practice. The UK rules stipulate:

♦ A full valuation should be performed at least every 5 years
♦ An interim valuation should be carried out in the third year after the full valuation
♦ Interim valuations should be carried out in the intervening years only where it is likely that there has been a material change in value.

Capitalization of borrowing costs

When a property is purchased the price paid will include a recoupment by the seller of finance costs they have incurred during construction.

Consequently there is logic to allowing an entity constructing a large capital asset to capitalize the finance costs they incur.

In the UK there is no bespoke accounting standard on this subject, but guidance can be sought both from the Companies Act 1985 and FRS 15 tangible fixed assets. Subject to some restrictions these allow finance costs on capital projects to be expensed as incurred or capitalized; the latter being permitted when:

◆ finance costs are being incurred
◆ expenditures for the asset are being incurred
◆ activities that are necessary to get the asset ready for use are in progress.

Internationally a bespoke standard, IAS 23 *Borrowing Costs*, exists and currently allows the same choice between expensing and capitalization. However, at the time of publication amendments to this standard are being proposed that would make capitalization mandatory to the extent that the finance cost is directly attributable to the acquisition, production or construction of a qualifying asset. This change is part of the ongoing project between the IASB and the US FASB to converge their respective accounting practices.

It should be noted that based on existing standards there is one significant difference between UK and international practice.

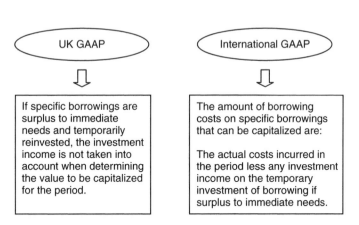

Government grants

Corporate legislation in the UK prohibits the direct deduction of capital grants from the carrying value of a fixed asset in the balance sheet – effectively requiring them to be shown as deferred income.

By contrast IAS 20 *Accounting for Government Grants and Disclosure of Government Assistance* allows either treatment.

Investment properties

There are separate rules under both international and UK GAAP for investment properties. The definition given to such assets under the two regimes is very similar.

UK GAAP	IAS GAAP
◆ Construction and development work complete ◆ Held for investment potential with rental income being negotiated at arms length Specifically excluded are ◆ properties owned and occupied by a company for its own purposes ◆ a property let to, and occupied by, another group company	◆ Property or land held to earn rentals and/or for capital gain It cannot be: ◆ owner occupied ◆ intended for sale in the ordinary course of business ◆ a property being constructed on behalf of third parties ◆ a property let to another group member. This is excluded in the context of the group accounts, but could still be classified as an investment property in the individual books of the lessor company

One major concern of UK companies viewing the transition to IAS/IFRS was that IAS 40 *Investment Property* did not allow a property interest, including land, held under an operating lease to be treated as an investment property. However, revisions to IAS 40 mean that this key difference has been eliminated.

However, some noteworthy discrepancies remain in the accounting treatment of investment properties that impact ratio analysis and other analytical tools used to review financial information. (See Figure 10.1)

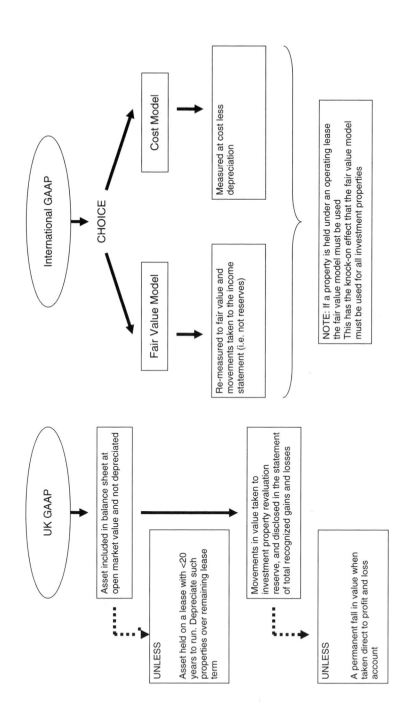

Figure 10.1 Investment properties – Comparison of accounting treatment

Box 10.2 Hammerson plc (2005) – Investment property disclosure note extract (International GAAP)

11 INVESTMENT AND DEVELOPMENT PROPERTIES

	Investment properties		Development properties			
	Valuation	Cost	Valuation	Cost	Valuation	Total Cost
	£m	£m	£m	£m	£m	£m
Balance at 1 January 2005	4,082.5	3,085.7	520.5	420.5	4,603.0	3,506.2
Exchange adjustment	(39.0)	(32.6)	(2.3)	(2.2)	(41.3)	(34.8)
Additions – Capital expenditure	77.9	77.9	130.8	130.8	208.7	208.7
– Asset acquisitions	279.6	279.6	2.1	2.1	281.7	281.7
– Corporate acquisitions	104.3	104.3	–	–	104.3	104.3
	461.8	461.8	132.9	132.9	594.7	594.7
Disposals	(193.3)	(214.9)	–	–	(193.3)	(214.9)
Transfers	95.9	59.8	(95.9)	(59.8)	–	–
Transfer to owner-occupied properties	(25.6)	(11.8)	–	–	(25.6)	(11.8)
Capitalised interest	0.2	0.2	21.0	21.0	21.2	21.2
Revaluation adjustment	575.5	–	197.5	–	773.0	–
Balance at 31 Decmber 2005	**4,958.0**	**3,348.2**	**773.7**	**512.4**	**5,731.7**	**3,860.6**

	Investment properties		Development properties			Total Cost
	Valuation £m	Cost £m	Valuation £m	Cost £m	Valuation £m	£m
Balance at 1 January 2004	3,650.0	2,911.3	300.5	262.1	3,950.5	3,173.4
Exchange adjustment	4.9	4.7	0.3	0.3	5.2	5.0
Additions – Capital expenditure	129.4	129.4	129.8	129.8	259.2	259.2
– Asset acquisitions	8.2	8.2	77.6	77.6	85.8	85.8
– Corporate acquisitions	285.5	285.5	–	–	285.5	285.5
	423.1	423.1	207.4	207.4	630.5	630.5
Disposals	(348.2)	(322.4)	–	–	(348.2)	(322.4)
Transfers	63.6	63.6	(63.6)	(63.6)	–	–
Capitalised interest	5.4	5.4	14.3	14.3	19.7	19.7
Revaluation adjustment	283.7	–	61.6	–	345.3	–
Balance at 31 December 2004	4,082.5	3,085.7	520.5	420.5	4,603.0	3,506.2

All properties are stated at market value as at 31 December 2005, valued by professionally qualified external valuers. In the United Kingdom, office properties and the group's interests in the Birmingham Alliance properties were valued by DTZ Debenham Tie Leung, Chartered Surveyors, and all other retail properties were valued by Donaldsons, Chartered Surveyors. In France and Germany, the group's properties were valued by Cushman & Wakefield Healey & Baker, Chartered Surveyors. The valuations have been prepared in accordance with the Appraisal and Valuation Standards of the Royal Institution of Chartered Surveyors and with IVA 1 of the International Valuation Standards. Valuation fees are based on a fixed amount agreed between the group and the valuers and are independent of the portfolio value. Summaries of the valuers' reports are available on the Company's website www.hammerson.co.uk.

At 31 December 2005 the total amount of capitalised interest included in development properties was £34.7 million (31 December 2004: £17.9 million) calculated using the group's average cost of borrowings.

Main sources of guidance

UK GAAP

- ◆ SSAP 4 *Accounting for Government Grants*
- ◆ SSAP 19 *Accounting for Investment Properties*
- ◆ FRS 15 *Tangible Fixed Assets*
- ◆ Companies Act 1985.

International GAAP

- ◆ IAS 16 *Property, Plant and Equipment*
- ◆ IAS 20 *Accounting for Government Grants and Disclosure of Government Assistance*
- ◆ IAS 23 *Borrowing Costs*
- ◆ IAS 40 *Investment Property*.

Key Facts

1. Companies have the choice of adopting a policy of revaluing tangible non-current assets, but this must be applied by class (i.e. cherry-picking is not allowed). This policy is permitted under UK GAAP and international GAAP, but the latter benchmarks to fair value whereas UK GAAP uses value in use.

2. Capitalization of borrowing costs is allowed. However, only international GAAP allows the offset of reinvestment income on specific borrowings that are surplus to immediate needs.

3. UK legislation prohibits the deduction of government grants directly from the carrying value of a non-current asset in the balance sheet whereas such treatment is permitted internationally.

4. Under international GAAP investment properties can be accounted for using the fair value model or the cost model. Whichever choice is made it must be used for all investment policies and applied consistently.
   UK GAAP does not permit an equivalent to the cost model.

5. Unless the cost model is applied investment properties are not depreciated under either accounting regime.

6. International GAAP requires all revisions to fair value to be taken to the income statement, but UK GAAP treats revisions to value as a movement on an investment property revaluation reserve unless they are deemed to be permanent when they become a profit and loss account entry.

Intangible Assets

Setting expectations

Intangible assets represent one of the greatest challenges in accounting as their value can be considerable, but their lack of physical substance can make proof of their existence and true worth difficult to validate.

The nature of these assets can be seen from their formal definition:

UK GAAP (FRS 10 *Goodwill and Intangible Assets*)

> A non-financial fixed asset that does not have physical substance, but is identifiable and is controlled by the entity through custody or legal rights

International GAAP (IAS 38 *Intangible Assets*)

> Identifiable non-monetary assets without physical substance

The variety of intangible assets is considerable and includes patents, royalty agreements, franchises, intellectual property, licences and goodwill. To streamline our understanding of the significant changes arising from the transition to international accounting rules, we will consider three broad categories.

1. Goodwill
2. Other intangibles
3. Research and development

Goodwill

Internally generated

Irrespective of the accounting system used, internally generated goodwill such as a reputation for good service built up over many years cannot be recognized as an asset in the balance sheet. It is not separately identifiable from the other assets of the business, and as such it would be impossible to accurately measure its value.

Goodwill arising on an acquisition

Often representing a significant proportion of balance-sheet assets this asset can be recognized as it has effectively been purchased as a component of the consideration paid by the acquirer. However, this does not imply that purchased goodwill is easily identified as there are other intangibles such as brands and publishing titles where the dividing line between their classification as a separate asset and an integral part of goodwill is wafer thin.

Under UK GAAP purchased goodwill is the difference between the fair value of the consideration given and the fair value of the identifiable net assets acquired. International GAAP puts greater emphasis on goodwill as a residual number, and it is assumed that the acquirer will make every effort to identify every other asset acquired; there is an acceptance that in achieving this objective greater judgement will have to be exercised in the identification process. This is highlighted by a closer examination of how goodwill is derived.

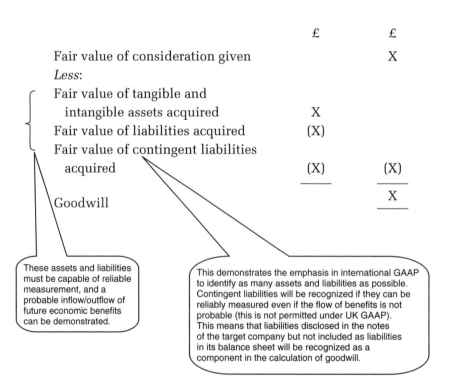

	£	£
Fair value of consideration given		X
Less:		
Fair value of tangible and intangible assets acquired	X	
Fair value of liabilities acquired	(X)	
Fair value of contingent liabilities acquired	(X)	(X)
		X
Goodwill		

These assets and liabilities must be capable of reliable measurement, and a probable inflow/outflow of future economic benefits can be demonstrated.

This demonstrates the emphasis in international GAAP to identify as many assets and liabilities as possible. Contingent liabilities will be recognized if they can be reliably measured even if the flow of benefits is not probable (this is not permitted under UK GAAP). This means that liabilities disclosed in the notes of the target company but not included as liabilities in its balance sheet will be recognized as a component in the calculation of goodwill.

The accounting treatment of purchased goodwill after recognition is the area of greatest contrast between UK and international GAAP.

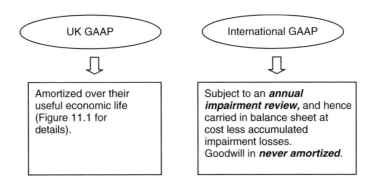

Figure 11.1 Treatment of purchased intangibles under UK GAAP subsequent to initial recognition

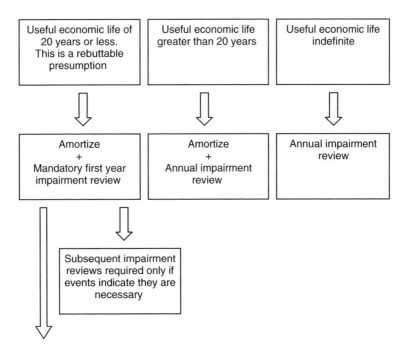

Illustration 11.1 Balfour Beatty plc (2004) – Accounting policy note extract

Goodwill treatment →

b) Basis of consolidation
The Group accounts include the accounts of the Company and its subsidiary undertakings, together with the Group's share of the results of joint ventures and associates drawn up to 31 December each year. The results of subsidiaries, joint ventures and associates acquired or sold in the year are consolidated from the respective date of acquisition or to the respective date of disposal. In accordance with FRS 10 "Goodwill and Intangible Assets", with effect from 1 January 1998, goodwill, being the excess of the fair value of consideration over the fair value of net assets acquired, arising on the acquisition of subsidiaries, joint ventures and associates is capitalized and amortised through the profit and loss account over the Directors' estimate of its economic useful life of up to 20 years. Goodwill arising before 1 January 1998 has been eliminated against reserves and is included in the profit and loss account at the time of the disposal of the business to which it relates.
   The Group's share of the net assets of contracting joint arrangements is included under each relevant heading within the balance sheet.

1.14 Goodwill
Goodwill represents the excess of the fair value of consideration over the fair value of the identifiable assets and liabilities acquired, arising on the acquisition of subsidiaries and other business entities, joint ventures and associates. Goodwill on acquisitions of subsidiaries and other business entities is included in non-current assets. Goodwill on acquisitions of joint ventures and associates is included in investments in joint ventures and associates.
   Goodwill is reviewed annually for impairment and is carried at cost less accumulated impairment losses. Goodwill is included when determining the profit or loss on subsequent disposal of the business to which it relates.
   Goodwill arising on acquisitions before the date of transition to IFRS has been retained at the previous UK GAAP amounts subject to being tested for impairment at that date. Goodwill written off or negative goodwill credited to reserves under UK GAAP prior to 1998 has not been reinstated and is not included in determining any subsequent profit or loss on disposal.

We will consider special rules relating specifically to the transition to IFRS in a later chapter looking at the detail of IFRS 1 *First-time Adoption of International Financial Reporting Standards*.

Illustration 11.2 Balfour Beatty (2005) – Accounting policy note extract (International GAAP)

Negative goodwill

The frequency of occasions when the consideration given is less than the fair value of the identifiable net assets of a business is very rare, and when it does occur the initial response should be to recheck the figures.

If such a discount on acquisition is genuine, international accounting practice requires it to be credited to the profit and loss account (i.e. income statement). The technical reason for this being that it does not meet the definition of a liability as specified by the IASBs Framework, and hence cannot be shown as such in the balance sheet.

Under UK GAAP negative goodwill is taken to the balance sheet and disclosed within fixed assets immediately below any positive goodwill that has arisen from other acquisitions. This 'negative' asset is then released to the profit and loss account in accordance with the following guidelines:

♦ Amounts equivalent to the fair value of the non-monetary assets (i.e. fixed assets and stock) acquired is released to the profit and loss account over the life of those assets.
♦ Any remaining balance is released over the periods expected to benefit.

Other intangibles

Although there are some subtle distinctions in the technical wording, the accounting treatment of other purchased intangibles is broadly similar under both accounting regimes. The assets are recognized in the balance sheet and then amortized over their useful economic lives unless indicators of impairment come to the attention of management whereupon these must be considered and asset values written down if appropriate.

Box 11.1 GlaxoSmithKline plc (2005) – Accounting policy extract (International GAAP)

Intangible assets

Intangible assets are stated at cost less provisions for amortisation and impairments.

Licences, patents, know-how and marketing rights separately acquired or acquired as part of a business combination are amortised over their estimated useful lives from the time they are available for use. The estimated useful lives for determining the amortisation charge are reviewed annually, and take into account the estimated time it takes to bring the compounds or products to market. Any development costs incurred by the Group and associated with acquired licences, patents, know-how or marketing rights are written off to the income statement when incurred,

---

unless the criteria for recognition of an internally generated intangible asset are met.

Brands are valued independently as part of the fair value of businesses acquired from third parties where the brand has a value which is substantial and long-term and where the brands can be sold separately from the rest of the businesses acquired. Brands are amortised over their estimated useful lives, except where it is considered that the useful economic life is indefinite.

Prior to 1998, acquired minor brands and similar intangibles were eliminated in the Group balance sheet against reserves in the year of acquisition.

The costs of acquiring and developing computer software for internal use and internet sites for external use are capitalised as intangible fixed assets where the software or site supports a significant business system and the expenditure leads to the creation of a durable asset. ERP systems software is amortised over seven years and other computer software over three to five years.

Irrespective of the accounting system used, the subject of internally generated intangibles remains one of the most contentious with key difficulties being the identification of a date when they come into existence and determining if they are capable of reliable measurement. Unless prudence is exercised there is clearly scope for a creative accountant as it would be difficult to prove or disprove the value associated with an asset.

Under UK GAAP the rules specify that an internally generated intangible other than goodwill can only be recognized as an asset if it has a readily ascertainable market value (i.e. there is an active market in equivalent assets that can act as a benchmark for valuation).

Internationally internally generated intangibles are caught by rules relating to research and development.

Research and development

In the UK this subject has its own bespoke accounting standard SSAP 13 *Accounting for Research and Development*, and is centred on the traditional view of this activity.

International GAAP gives a conceptually broader interpretation of research and development to capture all internally generated intangibles other than goodwill. No distinction is drawn between pure and applied research with all such costs being expensed.

Development costs can only be capitalized if conditions broadly similar to UK GAAP are met, but the key difference is that when the conditions are met the development costs must be capitalized, this is not an option.

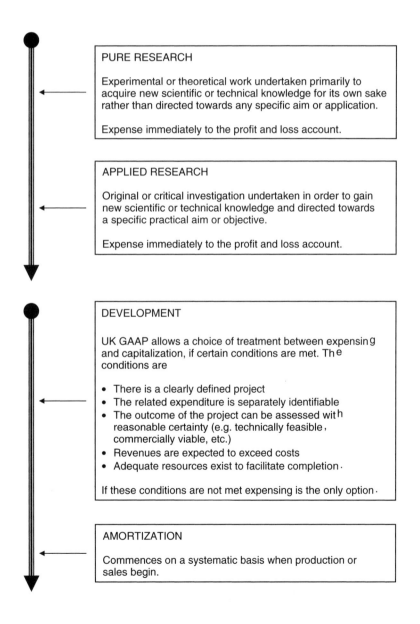

PURE RESEARCH

Experimental or theoretical work undertaken primarily to acquire new scientific or technical knowledge for its own sake rather than directed towards any specific aim or application.

Expense immediately to the profit and loss account.

APPLIED RESEARCH

Original or critical investigation undertaken in order to gain new scientific or technical knowledge and directed towards a specific practical aim or objective.

Expense immediately to the profit and loss account.

DEVELOPMENT

UK GAAP allows a choice of treatment between expensing and capitalization, if certain conditions are met. The conditions are

- There is a clearly defined project
- The related expenditure is separately identifiable
- The outcome of the project can be assessed with reasonable certainty (e.g. technically feasible, commercially viable, etc.)
- Revenues are expected to exceed costs
- Adequate resources exist to facilitate completion.

If these conditions are not met expensing is the only option.

AMORTIZATION

Commences on a systematic basis when production or sales begin.

Box **11.2** GlaxoSmithKline plc (2005) – Accounting policy extract (International GAAP)

Research and development

Research and development expenditure is charged to the income statement in the period in which it is incurred. Development expenditure is capitalised when the criteria for recognising an asset are met, usually when a regulatory filing has been made in a major market and approval is considered highly probable. Property, plant and equipment used for research and development is depreciated in accordance with the Group's policy.

Illustration of IAS GAAP

Box **11.3** GlaxoSmithKline plc (2005) – Intangible asset note

16. Goodwill

	2005 £m	2004 £m
Cost at 1st January	**304**	294
Exchange adjustments	**10**	11
Additions through business combinations	**383**	–
Disposals	**(1)**	–
Assets written off	–	(1)
Cost at 31st December	**696**	304
Net book value at 1st January	**304**	294
Net book value at 31st December	**696**	304

The additions for the year comprise £357 million on the acquisition of ID Biomedical Corporation and £26 million on the acquisition of Corixa Corporation. See Note 34 for further details.

Goodwill is not amortised but is tested for impairment at least annually. Value in use calculations are generally utilised to calculate recoverable amount. Value in use is calculated as the net present value of the projected risk-adjusted, post-tax cash flows of the cash generating unit in which the goodwill is contained, applying a discount rate of the Group post-tax weighted average cost of capital of 3%, adjusted where appropriate for country specific risks. This approximates to applying a pre-tax discount rate to pre-tax cash flows.

17. Other intangible assets

	Computer software £m	Licenses, patents, etc. £m	Brands £m	Total £m
Cost at 1st January 2004	541	1,059	1,169	2,769
Exchange adjustments	(6)	(39)	(25)	(70)
Additions	77	449	–	526
Disposals	(9)	(1)	(1)	(11)
Assets written off	(5)	(19)	–	(24)
Reclassifications from property, plant and equipment	11	–	–	11
Cost at 31st December 2004	609	1,449	1,143	3,201
Exchange adjustments	13	72	41	126
Additions	62	207	–	269
Additions through business combinations	–	816	–	816
Disposals	1	(29)	–	(28)
Assets written off	(10)	(43)	–	(53)
Reclassifications from property, plant and equipment	10	–	–	10
Cost at 31st December 2005	685	2,472	1,184	4,341
Amortisation at 1st January 2004	(234)	(202)	–	(436)
Exchange adjustments	3	11	–	14
Provision for the year	(93)	(75)	–	(168)
Disposals	9	–	–	9
Assets written off	4	1	–	5
Reclassifications from property, plant and equipment	(3)	–	–	(3)
Amortisation at 31st December 2004	(314)	(265)	–	(579)
Exchange adjustments	(6)	(21)	–	(27)
Provision for the year	(85)	(109)	–	(194)
Disposals	–	5	–	5
Assets written off	7	5	–	12
Reclassifications from property, plant and equipment	(1)	–	–	(1)

Amortisation at 31st December 2005	(399)	(385)	–	(784)
Impairment at 1st January 2004	(22)	(58)	(23)	(103)
Exchange adjustments	–	1	1	2
Impairment losses	(1)	(8)	–	(9)
Disposals	–	–	1	1
Impairment at 31st December 2004	(23)	(65)	(21)	(109)
Exchange adjustments	–	(2)	(2)	(4)
Impairment losses	(1)	(60)	(1)	(62)
Assets written off	1	–	–	1
Impairment at 31st December 2005	(23)	(127)	(24)	(174)
Total amortisation and impairment at 31st December 2004	(337)	(330)	(21)	(688)
Total amortisation and impairment at 31st December 2005	(422)	(512)	(24)	(958)
Net book value at 1st January 2004	285	799	1,	2,230
Net book value at 31st December 2004	272	1,119	1,122	2,513
Net book value at 31st December 2005	263	1,960	1,160	3,383

Amortisation and impairment has been charged through Research and development, and Selling, general and administration. At 31st December 2005, the net book value of computer software included £24 million that had been internally generated.

The additions through business combinations in the year of £816 million comprise £701 million from the acquisition of ID Biomedical Corporation and £115 million from the acquisition of Corixa Corporation (see Note 34). Other additions to licences and patents in the year relate to the purchase of development and commercialisation rights for Botox in certain territories acquired from Allergan and various other compounds rights (see Note 35).

Brands comprise a portfolio of products acquired with the acquisitions of Sterling Winthrop Inc. in 1994, and The Block Drug Company in 2001. The net book values of the major brands are as follows:

	2005 £m	2004 £m
Panadol	340	322
Sensodyne	230	226
Polident	97	96
Corega	87	85
Poligrip	60	59
Solpadeine	56	57
Others	290	277
	1,160	1,122

Each of these brands is considered to have an indefinite life, given the strength and durability of the brand and the level of marketing support. The brands are in relatively stable and profitable market sectors, and their size, diversification and market shares mean that the risk of market-related factors causing a shortening of the brands' lives is considered to be relatively low. The Group is not aware of any material legal, regulatory, contractual, competitive, economic or other factor which could limit their useful lives. Accordingly, they are not amortised. Each brand is tested annually for impairment applying a fair value less costs to sell methodology and using five year post-tax cash flow forecasts with a terminal value calculation and applying a discount rate of the Group post-tax weighted average cost of capital of 8%, adjusted where appropriate for country-specific risks. This approximates to applying a pre-tax discount rate to pre-tax cash flows.

The main assumptions include future sales prices and volumes, product contribution and the future development expenditure required to maintain the products marketability and registration in the relevant jurisdiction and the product's life. These assumptions are reviewed as part of management's budgeting and strategic planning cycle for changes in market conditions and product erosion, through generic competition.

Main sources of guidance

UK GAAP

- SSAP 13 *Accounting for Research and Development Costs*
- FRS 10 *Goodwill and Intangible Assets.*

International GAAP

◆ IAS38 *Intangible Assets.*
◆ IFRS 3 *Business Combinations.*

Key Facts

1. Internally generated goodwill can never be recognized as a balance-sheet asset under UK or international GAAP.
2. Under UK GAAP purchased goodwill is capitalized and then amortized over its useful economic life. In rare circumstances the latter may be deemed indefinite and the asset will be subject to an annual impairment review.

   Internationally purchased goodwill is never amortized. Standard practice is to conduct an annual impairment review and write asset values down as appropriate.
3. Under international accounting rules negative goodwill (i.e. a discount on acquisition) is credited to the income statement and never recognized in the balance sheet. This conflicts with UK GAAP where it is recognized in the balance sheet within the fixed assets section and amortized to the profit and loss account.
4. Other purchased intangibles have a similar treatment under both regimes (i.e. capitalization and amortization).
5. Internally generated intangible assets, other than goodwill, are rarely recognized. Under UK GAAP such recognition is only permitted if the asset has a readily ascertainable market value, whereas international rules place greater emphasis upon the conditions that permit the capitalization of development costs.
6. Research costs are always expensed.
7. Development costs can be capitalized under UK GAAP if qualifying criteria are met. Internationally subtlety different criteria are used, but the key difference is that when these have been met there is no choice – capitalization is mandatory.

Asset Impairment

Setting expectations

The principle of prudence dictates that assets should not be carried in the balance sheet of a company at a figure in excess of their recoverable amount. Both the accounting systems we are considering adhere to this principle, and require the carrying value of an asset to be derived by consideration of:

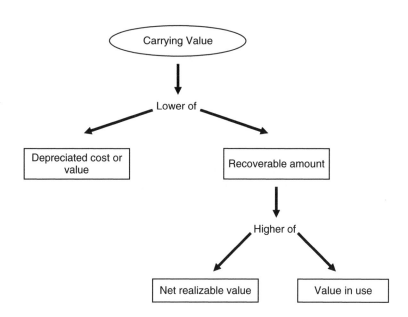

International terminology refers to net realizable value as fair value less costs to sell (e.g. stamp duty) but the terms are synonymous in practice. Value in use is always a difficult concept because it involves estimation of future cash flows generated by the asset and then discounting these to identify a present value.

Although there is a lot of common ground in the concepts underpinning impairment, more differences arise when looking at their application. With the exception of large and unique assets it would not be practical to ask management to conduct individual impairment reviews on every long-term asset in the business. Clearly assets need to be grouped but what are appropriate groupings, and if an impairment is identified how should it be allocated to the assets within the group?

Grouping assets and impairment allocation

Both IAS 36 *Impairment of Assets* and FRS 11 *Impairment of Fixed Assets and Goodwill* give examples of indicators that might suggest that an asset has been impaired. Neither listing is exhaustive and hence different inclusions would not be indicative of differences in accounting practice.

NOTE: IAS 36 does specifically include an indicator based on market capitalization which is not seen within UK GAAP.

Namely if the carrying amount of an entity's net assets exceeds its market capitalization there are suggestions of a lack of synergy and potential impairment.

However, prior to undertaking an impairment review it is usual to aggregate assets to facilitate the process.

UK GAAP – Income Generating Units [IGU]

A group of assets, liabilities and associated goodwill that generates income that is largely independent of the entity's other income streams. The assets and liabilities include those directly involved in generating income and an appropriate portion of those used to generate more than one income stream.

International GAAP – Cash-generating Units [CGU]

The smallest identifiable group of assets that generates cash inflows that are largely independent of the cash inflows from other assets or groups of assets.

If at the conclusion of the review of the IGU/CGU an impairment has been identified then it needs to be allocated across the assets contained within the grouping unless impairment to specific assets can be determined, and remembering to never reduce an individual asset to below its net realizable value. It is at this point that there is a divergence in accounting practice and to appreciate its potential significance we must recognize that many CGU/IGU will have three component parts.

1. An allocation of capitalized goodwill
2. Other intangibles assets (e.g. patents)
3. Tangible fixed (i.e. non-current) assets.

The differences lie in the order of impairment allocation (see Figure 12.1).

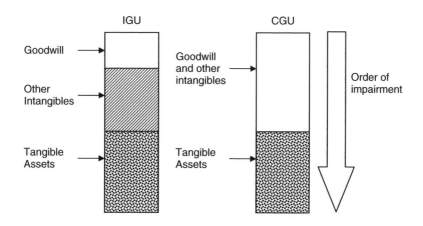

Figure 12.1 The allocation of an impairment to assets within a IGU/CGU

Under international GAAP no distinction is drawn between the goodwill and other intangibles thereby affecting the distribution of an impairment allocation compared to UK GAAP.

Value in use – discount rates

The calculation of value in use is heavily dependent upon the discount rate used to derive present values. Both UK GAAP and international practice recommend a pre-tax rate but guidance on its derivation differ.

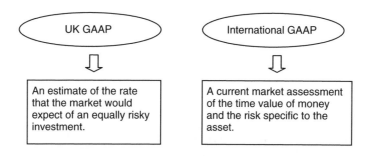

Value in use – look-back tests

Look-back testing is a feature unique to UK GAAP and requires an entity to retrospectively verify the accuracy of cash flow forecasts used in the derivation of value in use when this forms the basis of the recoverable amount.

This is to prevent management using an over-estimate of cash flows to avoid an impairment. If a look-back test identifies a previously unrecognized impairment then this must be recognized immediately.

Reversal of impairment

Both UK and international standards allow the reversal of impairments to tangible fixed assets. Such reversals are capped at the depreciated carrying value that would have been recorded if the impairment had never occurred.

However, UK and international practice do differ on the reversal of impairments made to goodwill and intangibles.

◆ FRS 11 *Impairment of Fixed Assets and Goodwill* only allows the reversal of impairments to intangible assets under very restricted circumstances, namely
  – The original impairment was caused by an external event
  – Subsequent external events subsequently reverse the original event in a way that could not have been foreseen at the date of the original impairment.
◆ IAS 36 *Impairment of Assets* prohibits the reversal of impairments to goodwill.
◆ IAS 36 allows the reversal of impairment to other intangible assets based on a similar criteria to that used for tangible assets (i.e. a change in the estimates used to determine the recoverable amount).

Main sources of guidance

UK GAAP

◆ FRS 11 *Impairment of Fixed Assets and Goodwill*

International GAAP

◆ *IAS 36 Impairment of Assets*

Key Facts

1. The model for asset impairment is common to UK and international GAAP requiring assets to be held in the balance sheet at the lower of their carrying value and the recoverable amount. The latter being the higher of the value in use and the net realizable value.

2. Groupings of assets under UK GAAP are referred to income-generating equivalents whereas the international equivalents are cash-generating units.

3. Under UK GAAP impairments are allocated against the assets contained in an IGU in a prescribed order, namely goodwill, then other intangibles and finally tangible assets. Under international rules goodwill and other intangibles are combined to form a single class.

4. Value in use is based on pre-tax discount rates, but there are subtle differences in the derivation of this rate that could impact the value calculated.

5. UK GAAP uses look-back tests to ensure that estimates made of future cash flows used within value-in-use calculations were not overstated.

6. IAS 36 does not allow the reversal of impairments made to goodwill.

Leasing

Setting expectations

Leasing is now a popular and widely accepted method of financing access to large capital assets, and although there is a wide variety of lease contracts accountants have historically always placed them under two categories.

1. Operating Leases
2. Finance leases (known as capital leases under some jurisdictions).

The essence of lease accounting both under UK GAAP and international GAAP is based on the principle of commercial substance prevailing over strict legal form. This is a double-edged sword as it ensures that legal dogma does not reduce the transparency of financial statements and yet simultaneously provides a potential opportunity for creative accounting in the guise of off-balance sheet finance.

An operating lease is the equivalent of a short-term rental whereby the bulk of the risks and rewards associated with ownership remain with the lessor. Hence substance and legal form are similar with the asset being recorded on the balance sheet of the lessor, whilst the lessee simply records an expense equivalent to the aggregate of the lease payments spread evenly over the lease term; hence cash flows and expenses may not be equal. It is this aspect that concerns many commentators on accounting as the absence of the asset and obligations contracted for future lease rentals lie outside the lessee's financial statements and are said to be off-balance sheet.

For a company that has net assets there are considerable attractions of off-balance sheet financing.

Example 13.1

Off-balance-sheet finance

A company requires a new capital asset that has a purchase price of £100,000, but the management team are undecided about the relative merits of outright purchase funded by additional debt compared to leasing the asset under an operating lease.

The company already has long-term borrowings from the bank who have included a gearing covenant in the loan agreement which stipulates that company gearing cannot exceed one.

The company currently has assets of £500,000 and liabilities of £200,000.

Operating Lease		Purchase
£500,000	Assets	£600,000
£200,000	Liabilities	£300,000
£300,000	Equity	£300,000
$\dfrac{200,000}{300,000} = 0.67$	Gearing	$\dfrac{300,000}{300,000} = 1.0$

Using an operating lease keeps the gearing substantially below the critical threshold and hence company funding is not threatened.

Under the terms of a finance lease legal title rests with the lessor but the risks and rewards of ownership are substantially transferred to the lessee. Consequently the asset is recorded in the books of the lessee as a fixed asset, and liabilities are increased by the value of the outstanding capital obligation; finance costs cannot be recognized until they fall due.

Box 13.1 Dairy Crest Group plc (2006) – Non-current asset finance lease disclosures (International GAAP)

10 Property, plant and equipment (continued)

Consolidated	Land and buildings £m	Vehicles, plant and equipment £m	Assets in the course of construction £m	Total £m
Cost				
At 1 April 2004	168.9	313.2	58.9	541.0
Additions at cost	11.1	11.0	17.6	39.7
Acquisitions	–	–	0.1	0.1
Disposals	(17.3)	(79.4)	–	(96.7)
Transfers and reclassifications	12.4	45.0	(57.4)	–
Exchange adjustments	–	0.4	–	0.4
At 31 March 2005	175.1	290.2	19.2	484.5

Accumulated depreciation				
At 1 April 2004	57.7	168.2	–	225.9
Charge for the year	5.6	28.3	–	33.9
Asset write-downs	–	(0.2)	–	(0.2)
Disposals	(14.2)	(78.2)	–	(92.4)
Exchange adjustments	–	0.3	–	0.3
At 31 March 2005	49.1	118.4	–	167.5
Net book amount at 31 March 2005	126.0	171.8	19.2	317.0
Net book amount at 31 March 2004	111.2	145.0	58.9	315.1

Capitalised leases included in vehicles, plant and equipment comprise:	2006 £m	2005 £m
Cost	51.6	51.4
Accumulated depreciation	(32.0)	(30.3)
Net book amount	19.6	21.1

Leased assets are pledged as security for the related finance lease liability (see Note 26).

Both the IASB and the Accounting Standards Board (ASB) in the UK have published Discussion Papers looking at the merits of a new approach to lease accounting. If implemented this would see the effective demise of the operating lease as all assets and liabilities arising under lease agreements would have to be recognized at fair value in the books of the lessee.

Determining lease classification

In the light of the significantly different accounting approaches to operating and finance leases one immediate question should spring to mind.

Is it possible that the designation of a lease could be different under international accounting rules such that an operating lease under UK GAAP would be treated as a finance lease internationally?

The answer is yes, and hence it is vital that we understand how this could happen as it is fundamental to the recognition and presentation of assets and liabilities in the financial statements.

We know that the key feature of a finance lease is that the risks and rewards normally associated with ownership have been transferred to the lessee, although legal title remains with the lessor. However, this apparent commonality hides a different approach to determining when the risks and rewards have moved.

UK GAAP

Under SSAP 21 *Accounting for Leases and Hire Purchase Contracts* there is a rebuttable presumption that risks and rewards have been transferred, if a yes answer can be given to the following:

Is the present value of the minimum lease payments	>	90% of the fair value of the leased asset?

In layman's terms a yes answer implies that the lessee will effectively pay an amount equivalent to the purchase price of the asset.

International GAAP

This does not contain a direct equivalent to the 90 per cent test, but requires consideration be given to a series of judgemental criteria.

- ◆ The lease transfers ownership of the asset to the lessee at the end of the lease.
- ◆ The lessee has the option to purchase the asset at a price that is expected to be significantly lower than the fair value at the date

the option becomes exercisable for it to be reasonably certain, at the inception of the lease, that the option will be exercised.

◆ The lease term is for the major part of the economic life of the asset even if title is not transferred.

◆ At the inception of the lease the present value of the minimum lease payments amounts to at least substantially all of the fair value of the leased asset.

◆ The leased assets are of a specialized nature such that only the lessee can use them without major modifications being made.

[IAS 17 para 10]

One consequence of these differences is an increased probability of a lease being designated as a finance lease resulting in a deterioration of key ratios when making the transition to international GAAP.

Land and building issues

IAS 17 places greater emphasis on the treatment of leases for land and buildings, and requires a single lease to be split into the separate elements. There is a strong logic to this approach as land has an infinite life and hence it would be very unlikely that substantially all the risks and rewards of ownership will be transferred to the lessee; consequently the land element should be treated as an operating lease. The classification of the building element will be dependent upon the specific terms of the agreement.

Operating lease disclosures

As always there are subtle differences in the disclosure requirements of different countries dictated by national legislation and the way it interacts with best accounting practice. The aim of this book is not to look at every miniscule difference, but with reference to operating leases there is one disparity of which you must be aware.

SSAP 21 requires a note disclosure that shows the non-cancellable operating lease payments which the lessee is committed to make during the next year. These payments are analysed between leases expiring within 1 year, in the second to fifth years and those expiring after the fifth year. Operating leases relating to land and buildings must be shown separately from other leases (Box 13.2).

Box 13.2 Rentokil Initial plc (2004) – Operating lease commitments

The group has lease agreements in respect of properties, vehicles, plant and equipment, the payments for which extend over a number of years. The minimum annual rentals are:

	LAND AND BUILDINGS	OTHER OPERATING LEASES	TOTAL	TOTAL
	2004	2004	2004	2003
	£m	£m	£m	£m
Operating leases which expire:				
Within one year	3.7	3.3	7.0	5.0
Between two and five years	13.8	10.3	24.1	23.8
After five years	17.2	1.8	19.0	17.0
	34.7	15.4	50.1	45.8

By contract IAS 17 requires disclosure of the total future minimum lease payments under non-cancellable operating leases. Again there is a split proportionate to time (i.e. less than 1 year, 2–5 years and greater than 5 years), but the period now reflects when the payments are due rather than the unexpired term of the lease (Box 13.3).

Box 13.3 Rentokil Initial plc (2005) – Operating leases note

35. Operating leases

The group leases properties, vehicles, plant and equipment under non-cancellable operating lease agreements. The leases have varying terms, escalation clauses and renewal rights. The lease expenditure charged to the income statement during the year is disclosed in note 2.

The future aggregate minimum lease payments under non-cancellable operating leases are as follows:

	2005 £m	2004 £m
Not later than one year	5.6	6.2
Later than one year and not later than five years	20.0	20.7
Later than five years	14.3	17.5
	39.9	44.4

Allocation of finance costs

An important aspect of accounting for finance leases is the method for the recognition of finance costs.

When viewed from the perspective of the lessee both accounting regimes promote the actuarial method, but allow sum of digits as an approximation. The actuarial method ensures that the finance cost is proportionate to the outstanding capital liability, and hence straight-line recognition of finance costs is prohibited unless the amounts are immaterial to the financial statements.

Allocation of finance income by the lessor is more complex as it needs to take into account additional factors such as taxation and grants when calculating an actuarial rate. IAS 17 requires the actuarial pre-tax method to be used whereas UK GAAP stipulates the actuarial post-tax method.

Main sources of guidance

UK GAAP

◆ SSAP 21 *Accounting for Leases and Hire Purchase Contracts*

International GAAP

◆ IAS 17 *Leases*

Key Facts

1. UK GAAP bases lease classification primarily on the 90 per cent test, whereby if the present value of the minimum lease payments exceeds 90 per cent of the fair value of the leased asset there is a presumption that the lease is a finance lease. International GAAP does not have a directly equivalent test.

2. International GAAP requires a lease for land and buildings to be split into its constituent parts. Leases for land are likely to represent operating leases as it is difficult to demonstrate that substantially all the risks and rewards of ownership have been passed to the lessee when the underlying asset has an indefinite life.

3. Disclosure of operating lease commitments differs with UK GAAP focussing on amounts falling due in the next year whereas IAS 17 requires disclosure of all future commitments under non-cancellable leases.

Stock and Long-term Contracts

Setting expectations

With the obvious exception of a different label, inventory replacing stock, the accounting treatment for this key asset is fundamentally identical. Hence stock/inventory is valued at the lower of cost and net realizable value.

Historically there was a divergence in treatment when considering the cost-flow strategies allowed under UK and international accounting rules. UK GAAP has always prohibited the use of LIFO (Last-In Last-Out), but a similar ban was only introduced to international GAAP in 2004. It is worthy of note that LIFO remains an acknowledged method in the US further demonstrating the difficulties which remain in producing a global GAAP.

UK long-term contracts appear more at odds with their international counterpart, construction contracts, for which there is a separate accounting standard. Closer examination reveals that the differences are again minor as will be proved by the following comparison.

What's in a name?

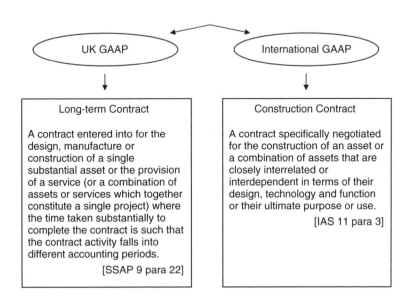

Internationally less emphasis is placed upon the concept of long term and hence it is possible that a company adopting IAS 11 will apply a percentage of completion methodology to the recognition of a short contract. In the UK it is more likely that a completed contract methodology would be used.

> NOTE: Remember that the term 'completed contract methodology' refers to circumstances when no profits are recognized during the life of a contract, but are taken in one 'hit' upon completion. This is a very prudent approach but results in a lack of matching of profits to activity for a longer contract.

Reduced disclosure

A common feature of many contracts accounted for using the percentage completion methodology is that revenues and costs recognized in the annual performance statement will not match the costs incurred or revenues billed. This leads to repercussions for the balance sheet.

Under UK GAAP these differences can be crystallized in four ways:

1. Actual costs incurred to date > Amounts recognized in cost of sales

⇨ | Work in progress (i.e. inventory) |

2. Actual costs incurred to date < Amounts recognized in cost of sales

⇨ | Creditors or provisions for a loss making contract |

3. Turnover > Payments on account

⇨ | Debtors |

4. Turnover < Payments on account

⇨ | Offset against any long-term contract balances and any excess disclosed within creditors as payments on account |

Presentation under international GAAP is more aggregated and draws no distinction between amounts recoverable on contracts and work in progress.

Box 14.1 Balfour Beatty plc (2005) – Construction contracts note (International GAAP)

19 Construction contracts
Contracts in progress at balance sheet date:

	2005	2004
	£m	£m
Due from customers for contract work	217	218
Due to customers for contract work	(274)	(264)
	(57)	(46)

The aggregate amount of costs incurred plus recognised profits (less recognised losses) for all contracts in progress at the balance sheet date was £13,368m (2004: £12,369m).

Main sources of guidance

UK GAAP

♦ SSAP 9 *Stocks and Long-term Contracts.*

International GAAP

♦ IAS 2 *Inventories*
♦ IAS 11 *Construction Contracts.*

Key Facts

1. For the purposes of reviewing financial statements there are no substantive differences in the treatment of stock/inventory under UK GAAP and international GAAP.
2. Differences on long-term contracts/construction contracts are generally minor, but there are potential disparities for 'shorter' contracts, and international GAAP gives more aggregated disclosures.

Taxation

Setting expectations

With the exception of potential confusion over the terminology used there are no significant differences in the accounting treatment for current tax; just remember that in the UK companies are subject to corporation tax whereas internationally the term 'income tax' is used to cover both the taxation of companies and individuals for this more specialized subject.

However, in spite of significant changes being made to UK GAAP in 2000 with the release of FRS 19 *Deferred Tax* there remain some noteworthy differences in accounting practice.

FRS 19 snapshot

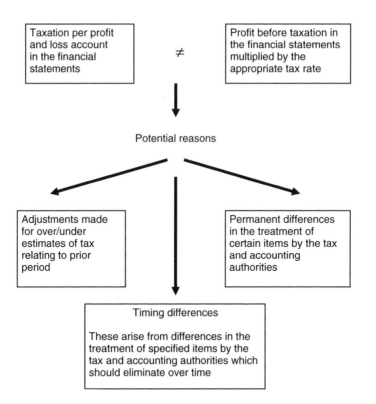

A classic example of a timing difference relates to the treatment of tangible fixed assets. Accountants depreciate such assets over their useful economic life, whereas the UK tax authorities effectively ignore depreciation, but in its place allow companies capital allowances that lower profits chargeable to corporation tax. The pattern of depreciation and capital and allowances are rarely the same thereby giving rise to a timing difference.

Deferred tax is the tax on timing differences, and represents a recognition of the impact on future tax of past events. The standard requires full provisioning subject to certain specific exemptions whereby tax is provided on all timing differences at the balance-sheet date.

IAS 12 – Temporary differences instead of timing differences

International practice has a balance-sheet focus and effectively considers the tax that would be payable if the company were liquidated today. Deferred tax is the tax on temporary differences which are the differences between the carrying value of an asset or liability in the balance sheet and its tax base. The latter representing the amount attributed to that asset/liability for tax purposes. As with UK GAAP the concept of full provisioning applies whereby tax is provided on the total value of the temporary differences at the balance-sheet date.

In a majority of cases the practical impact of calculating deferred taxation based on timing differences or temporary differences is nil with the same provision being made in the balance sheet. However, this will not always be the case and the differences can be very significant.

◆ All timing differences will always be classified as temporary differences
◆ Some temporary differences would not be classed as timing differences and hence this raises the spectre of larger deferred tax provisions under international accounting rules.

NOTE: A simple way in which to visualize the difference between the two approaches is that the international methodology adopts the prudent assumtion that 'the World stops spinning at the balance sheet date' and hence there will be no future events that might mitigate the tax charge.

Examples of such disparities between UK GAAP and international GAAP include the following.

Revaluations of non-monetary assets

When an asset is revalued the accountant recognizes this in the period it occurs, but the tax authorities only crystallize a chargeable gain when the asset is sold. Under UK GAAP if no binding sale agreement exists or rollover tax relief is available no provision would be made for deferred taxation. IAS 12 requires full provision for this temporary difference – its 'end of the World' approach implying the company will be liquidated and the asset sold thereby realizing the gain.

Unremitted earnings

IAS 12 makes provision for the deferred taxation arising on unremitted earnings from subsidiaries, branches, joint ventures and associates. By contrast UK GAAP only requires provision to the extent that such earnings have been accrued at the balance-sheet date or there is a binding agreement to distribute past earnings.

Fair value adjustments

International practice requires provision to be made for deferred tax on all fair value adjustments, except for non-deductible goodwill, whereas this is not required under FRS 19.

Discounting

International accounting practice prohibits the discounting of deferred tax balances. This practice is allowed under UK GAAP, but was rarely an option chosen in practice.

Box 15.1 J Sainsbury plc (2005) – Tax accounting policy note (UK GAAP)

Deferred tax

Provision for deferred tax is made in respect of all timing differences that have originated, but not reversed, by the balance sheet date. The provision for deferred tax is not discounted. Deferred tax assets are only recognised to the extent that it is considered more likely than not that they will be recovered. Deferred tax is not provided on unremitted earnings of subsidiaries, where no commitment to remit these earnings had been made.

Intragroup transactions

Taxation is levied against the profits of individual companies and consequently if one group company sells to another at a profit this will be taxed. However on consolidation to produce group financial statements intragroup trading and any associated unrealized profits are eliminated. This difference in accounting and tax treatment gives rise to a temporary/timing difference and has deferred tax consequences.

In calculating the resultant deferred tax a difference should be noted between UK GAAP and its international equivalent.

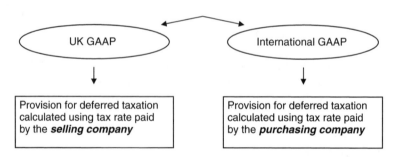

Deferred tax assets

Deferred tax assets typically arise through the existence of tax losses. As with any asset accounting, best practice requires a degree of prudence to be exercised when considering its recognition. Both FRS 19 and IAS 12 require an assessment to be made to determine the recoverability of this asset, but the criteria used are subtlety different with the result that a deferred tax asset is more likely to be recognized under the remit of IAS 12.

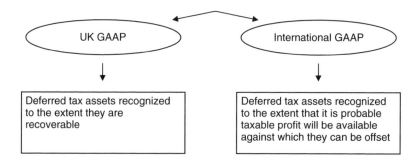

Both UK GAAP and international GAAP only allow the offset of deferred tax assets and liabilities in very restricted circumstances where there is a legally enforceable right of set off.

Disclosure

Most stakeholders who read a set of financial statements are unlikely to be tax experts, and so they require additional guidance on the derivation of the tax charge in comparison to the reported profits. UK GAAP restricts the reconciliation associated with this disclosure to the current tax charge only, whereas IAS 19 is more comprehensive and requires a reconciliation of the current and deferred tax charge with the tax a user would have expected to see (i.e. the reported profit multiplied by the appropriate tax rate).

Box 15.2   Balfour Beatty plc (2005) – Tax reconciliation (International GAAP)

9.2 Taxation reconciliation

	Group 2005 £m	Group 2004 £m	Company 2005 £m	Company 2004 £m
Profit before taxation	141	120	32	46
Less: Share of results of joint ventures and associates	(73)	(36)		
Group profit before taxation	68	84		

Tax on Group/Company profit before taxation at standard UK corporation tax rate of 30% (2004: 30%)	**20**	25	**10**	14
Effects of:				
Expenses not deductible for tax purposes including impairment of goodwill	**6**	11	–	4
Dividend income not taxable	–	–	**(19)**	(16)
Preference shares finance costs not deductible	**5**	–	**5**	–
Movement in deferred tax not recognized	**(3)**	–	–	–
Losses not available for offset	**9**	13	–	–
Higher/(lower) tax rates on foreign earnings	**3**	1	–	–
Disposal of investments and other assets not taxable	**(2)**	(1)	**(2)**	–
Advance corporation tax written back	–	(11)	–	(11)
Adjustments in respect of other periods	**(3)**	(10)	**(5)**	(7)
Total tax changes/(credit)	**35**	28	**(11)**	(16)

Main sources of guidance

UK GAAP

◆ FRS 19 *Deferred Tax*

International GAAP

◆ IAS 12 *Income Taxes*

Key Facts

1. Under UK GAAP deferred tax is the tax on timing differences whereas internationally it is the tax on temporary differences.

The international approach recognizes as temporary differences certain items (e.g. those relating to the revaluation of non-current assets) that would not constitute a timing difference in the UK. Hence UK companies making the transition to international rules would have expected to see an increase in their tax provisions.

2. Both systems adopt the principle of full provisioning.
3. IAS 12 prohibits the discounting of deferred tax balances.
4. When calculating the deferred tax attributable to intragroup transactions UK GAAP bases the provision on the tax rate applicable to the selling company whereas international GAAP refers to the tax regime of the purchaser.
5. UK GAAP is more restrictive in its recognition of deferred tax assets.
6. International GAAP requires a reconciliation of the entities' actual, current and deferred tax charge to the amount of tax that would have been payable applying the standard rate of tax to the pre-tax profits reported in the financial statements.

Retirement Benefits

Setting expectations

The pensions provided by companies to their employees come in many forms, but fundamentally these fall into two distinct classes.

1. Defined contribution schemes – Also known as money purchase schemes these are attractive to companies as they are easy to record, and more significantly it is the employees who bear the risk of poor performance by the pension fund established.

   The company's exposure is limited to their contractual commitment to pay an amount equal to a percentage of employee salary into the scheme. If the pension assets purchased with these funds perform poorly and result in a smaller pension, it is the former employee who suffers.

2. Defined benefit schemes – Also known as 'final salary schemes' these are becoming increasingly unattractive to employers as it is the company that now bears the risk of poor fund performance. In effect such schemes guarantee employees a percentage of their final salary as a pension – the exact percentage being linked to the number of years service they have provided to the employer.

   These schemes need regular actuarial review (usually every 3 years) when the professionals involved perform complex modelling to evaluate a range of future events and their impact on the funds required by the pension scheme to meet its obligations. The projections of the future that an actuary will need to be made include:

   ◆ Inflation
   ◆ Interest rates
   ◆ Numbers of people joining or leaving the scheme
   ◆ The average service life of employees
   ◆ Performance of capital markets.

Clearly this is not a job for the faint-hearted!

Both UK GAAP and its international equivalent use a balance-sheet approach when accounting for defined benefit schemes, and the approaches reflect many similarities (see Figure 16.1).

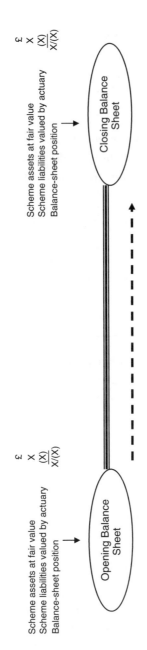

Scheme assets at fair value
Scheme liabilities valued by actuary
Balance-sheet position

X
(X)
X/(X)

Opening Balance Sheet

Scheme assets at fair value
Scheme liabilities valued by actuary
Balance-sheet position

X
(X)
X/(X)

Closing Balance Sheet

The movement from the opening to the closing position is partly explained by the following:

- Funds injected by the company to the scheme – increasing scheme assets
- Benefits paid to former employees – decreases assets and liabilities of the scheme
- Current service cost as established by the terms of the scheme – charged as an operating expense in the performance statement and increasing scheme liabilities
- Finance costs attributable to the progressive reversal of discounting on long-term liabilities – recognized as a finance cost in the performance statement and increasing scheme liabilities
- Expected return on assets – increasing scheme assets and bolstering profits in the performance statement.

BUT

It is unlikely the opening and closing positions will have been fully reconciled as however good the skills of the actuary there will have been deviations from the estimates they made (known as actuarial gains and losses). It is at this point that accounting practice starts to diverge.

Figure 16.1 Defined benefit pension schemes – Accounting basics

Accounting for actuarial gains and losses

Actuarial gains and losses represent the movement in the value of a pension fund that had not been anticipated in the estimates used by an actuary. The amounts involved can be substantial particularly when a dramatic World event leads to a crash in the capital markets.

In the UK these gains and losses are required to be taken, in full, directly to reserves and will be disclosed within the statement of total recognized gains and losses.

It should be noted that although FRS 17 *Retirement Benefits* was published in November 2000 full adoption was not mandatory until accounting periods beginning on or after 1 January 2005. This means that listed companies could continue to adhere to 'old' UK GAAP until they reached the transition period for the mandatory move to IFRS. Consequently they could bypass FRS 17.

Box 16.1 Cadbury Schweppes plc (2004) – Accounting policy note extract

(r) Pensions

The costs of providing pensions and other post-retirement benefits are charged to the profit and loss account on a consistent basis over the service lives of employees. Such costs are calculated by reference to actuarial valuations and variations from such regular costs are spread over the remaining service lives of the current employees. To the extent to which such costs do not equate with cash contributions, a provision or prepayment is recognised in the balance sheet.

The Group continues to use SSAP 24 'Accounting for Pension Costs' to account for pension costs, and provides the required transitional disclosures under FRS 17 'Retirement Benefits'.

The 'old' UK GAAP referred to above was SSAP 24 *Accounting for Pension Costs* and approached pension accounting from a profit and loss account perspective. A simple example of the consequences of using SSAP 24 is given in Example 16.1.

Example 16.1

Pension accounting using SSAP 24

XYZ plc operates a defined benefit pension scheme into which it makes regular contributions of £12 million per annum. In 1999 actuaries reviewed the scheme and identified a £20 million deficit, and it was agreed that in 2000 the company would make a one-off additional payment to make good the shortfall.

The average service life of employees in the scheme is 5 years.

Applying the concepts of SSAP 24 what is the impact of the deficit correction on the profit and loss account and balance sheet for 2000–2004?

Year	Cash £m	Profit and Loss Expense £m	Balance Sheet £m
1999	12	12	–
2000	32	16	16 Prepaid
2001	12	16	12 Prepaid
2002	12	16	8 Prepaid
2003	12	16	4 Prepaid
2004	12	16	–

The £20 million correction is spread evenly over the average remaining service life of employees in the scheme. An anomaly of this method is that the balance sheet reflects an asset, but this has arisen because there is a deficit on the scheme.

International accounting best practice as encapsulated by IAS 19 *Employee Benefits* allows three solutions to the treatment of actuarial gains and losses.

1. The actuarial gain or loss is recognized in full as it occurs. Recognition is not via the income statement, but via a statement of recognized income and expense. This method is effectively used by FRS 17 under UK GAAP.

Box 16.2 J Sainsbury plc (2006) – Accounting policy note extract

> **Employee benefits**
> **Pensions**
> The Group operates various defined benefit and defined contribution pension schemes for its employees. A defined benefit scheme is a pension plan that defines an amount of pension benefit that an employee will receive on retirement. A defined contribution scheme is a pension plan under which the Group pays fixed contributions into a separate entity.
>
> In respect of defined benefit pension schemes, the pension scheme deficit recognised in the balance sheet represents the difference between the fair value of the plan assets and the present value of the defined benefit obligation at the balance sheet date. The defined benefit obligation is actuarially calculated on an annual basis using the projected unit credit method. Plan assets are recorded at fair value.
>
> The income statement charge is split between an operating service cost and a financing charge, which is the net of interest cost on pension scheme liabilities and expected return on plan assets. Actuarial gains and losses are recognised in full in the period, in the statement of recognised income and expense.
>
> Payments to defined contribution pension schemes are charged as an expense as they fall due. Any contributions unpaid at the balance sheet date are included as an accrual as at that date. The Group has no further payment obligations once the contributions have been paid.

Actuarial gains and losses to be recognized in full

Statements of recognized income and expense are allowed by IAS 1 *Presentation of Financial Statements* as a representation of a statement of changes in equity.

Box 16.3 J Sainsbury plc (2006) – Statement of recognized income and expense

Statements of recognised income and expense
for the 52 weeks to 25 March 2006

		Group		Company	
	Note	2006 £m	2005 £m	2006 £m	2005 £m
Currency translation differences		2	(3)	–	–
Actuarial (losses)/gains on defined benefit pension schemes		(255)	128	–	–
Available-for-sale financial assets fair value movements		26	–	–	–

Cash flow hedges					
effective portion of fair value movements		1	–	–	–
transferred to income statement		(1)	–	–	–
Share-based payment tax deduction	9	5	–	–	–
Tax on items recognised directly in equity	9	68	(38)	–	–
Net (loss)/income recognised directly in equity		(154)	87	–	–
Profit for the financial year		58	188	153	350
Total recognised income and expense for the financial year		(96)	275	153	350
Attributable to:					
Equity holders of the parent		(90)	271	153	350
Minority interests		(6)	4	–	–
		(96)	275	153	350
Effect of changes in accounting policy on adoption of IAS 32 and IAS 39:	43				
Equity holders of the parent		(78)		(149)	
Minority interests		–		–	
		(78)		(149)	

2. The second method of accounting for actuarial gains and losses recognizes that actuarial estimates of pension scheme liabilities will never be an exact science. Consequently it calculates a 10 per cent corridor around the estimate, and does not require gains and losses that fall within this corridor to be recognized in the income statement.

NOTE: The 10 per cent corridor is the greater of:

◆ 10% of the present value of the defined benefit obligation; and
◆ 10% of the fair value of the plan assets.

These are as measured at the start of the accounting period and not at the end.

When the 10 per cent corridor is broken the excess is spread forward to the income statement over the average remaining service life of employees in the scheme.

The theoretical basis for this approach is often questioned, and it is possible that at a future date it might be banned by the IASB.

3. The final method allows actuarial gains and losses to be taken direct to the income statement at a faster rate than would occur when spreading over the average remaining service life of employees. Theoretically it allows all the gain or loss, including that which falls within the corridor, to be taken in a single period, but the dramatic impact this could have on reported performance would dissuade most management teams.

Valuing scheme assets

Historically UK GAAP and IAS have differed on the subject of quoted asset valuation.

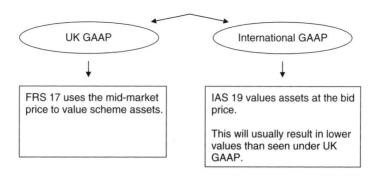

However, an amendment to FRS 17 effective from 6 April 2007 has aligned UK practice to use of the bid price.

Presentation

The amendment to FRS 17 referred to under asset valuation has also further aligned the presentation requirements of FRS 17 with international GAAP.

This has resulted in additional disclosures being required by FRS 17 such as:

♦ The principal actuarial assumptions used as at the balance-sheet date
♦ An analysis of the opening and closing scheme assets and liabilities showing separately the movements in each
♦ An analysis of scheme liabilities into amounts relating to unfunded schemes and those that are wholly or partially funded.

However, the need for other disclosures formally required by UK GAAP have been removed, including:

♦ the date of the most recent full-actuarial valuation
♦ how the underlying present value of scheme liabilities is effected by changes in demographic and financial assumptions
♦ the financial assumptions at the beginning of the period
♦ an analysis of the notes to the financial statements distinguishing the amount relating to the defined benefit asset or liability net of the related deferred tax.

Other presentational discrepancies exist between UK and international practice with the latter allowing greater flexibility on the proviso that when a presentational style has been selected it must be applied consistently. For example, IAS 19 does not specify if the current service cost, finance costs and expected returns on scheme assets should be presented separately or in aggregate.

IAS 19 – A broader emit

It should be noted that unlike its UK counterpart IAS 19 provides guidance on a wider range of employee benefits including:

♦ Other long-term benefits
♦ Short-term employee benefits
♦ Termination benefits.

Main sources of guidance

UK GAAP

◆ FRS 17 *Retirement Benefits*

International GAAP

◆ IAS 19 *Employee Benefits*

Key Facts

1. UK GAAP requires that actuarial gains and losses are recognized in full in the period they arise. They represent a reserve movement and are disclosed in the statement of total recognized gains and losses.
2. Internationally there are three methods allowed for the treatment of actuarial gains and losses. One is equivalent to the UK, another allows these gains and losses to be taken direct to the income statement and another uses a corridor approach whereby gains and losses in excess of the corridor are taken to the income statement over the period of the average remaining service life of employees in the scheme.
3. Until April 2007 the valuation of quoted assets differed between FRS 17 and IAS 19. This has now been unified so that both use the bid price.

Revenue Recognition

Setting expectations

UK GAAP offers only modest guidance on the subject of revenue recognition in the form of:

◆ Application Note G to FRS 5 *Reporting the Substance of Transactions*
◆ UITF Abstract 40 *Revenue Recognition and Service Contracts.*

You will recall from earlier in the text that a UITF represents the Urgent Issues Task Force.

By contrast the IASB has a full accounting standard, IAS 18 *Revenue*, on revenue recognition.

IAS 18 – a brief synopsis

The lack of formal guidance within UK GAAP means that it is not possible to make a direct comparison with international practice. However, it is useful to be aware of the key features of the latter which breaks revenue recognition into three areas.

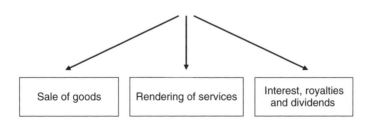

Sales of goods

Revenue should be recognized when all of the following conditions have been met:

◆ The entity has transferred to the buyer the significant risks and rewards of ownership of the goods.
◆ The entity contains neither continuing managerial involvement to the degree usually associated with ownership nor effective control over the goods sold.
◆ The amount of revenue can be measured reliably.
◆ It is probable that the economic benefits associated with the transaction will flow to the entity.

◆ The costs incurred or to be incurred in respect of the transaction can be measured reliably.

[IAS 18 para 14]

Rendering of services

The conditions to be met in these circumstances are

◆ The amount of revenue can be measured reliably.
◆ It is probable that the economic benefits associated with the transaction will flow to the entity.
◆ The stage of completion of the transaction at the balance-sheet date can be measured reliably.
◆ The costs incurred for the transaction and the costs to complete the transaction can be measured reliably.

[IAS 18 para 20]

Interest, royalties and dividends

Recognition should be made if:

◆ It is probable that the economic benefits associated with the transaction will flow to the entity.
◆ The amount of the revenue can be measured reliably.

For dividend recognition it is also necessary that:

◆ The shareholders' right to receive payment is established.

[IAS 18 para 29 and 30]

Main sources of guidance

International GAAP

◆ IAS 18 *Revenue*

Key Facts

1. UK GAAP lacks a stand-alone accounting standard on revenue recognition.

Group Accounts –
Acquisition Accounting

Setting expectations

The consolidation of subsidiaries and quasi-subsidiaries is a large subject, but the good news is that the fundamental mechanics involved in the preparation of group accounts remains the same under UK and international GAAP. However 'bear traps' do remain such as differences in the definition of a subsidiary, and it is these we need to tackle if misunderstandings are to be avoided.

What is a subsidiary?

In 2004 the definition of a subsidiary under the UK Companies Act 1985 was amended with the result that some of the disparity between UK and international recognition of this investment type was narrowed. However, differences remain.

UK GAAP

Subsidiary status is applicable if from the perspective of the parent any of the following apply:

- ◆ It holds a majority of the voting rights in the undertaking.
- ◆ It is a member of the undertaking and has the right to appoint or remove directors holding a majority of the voting rights at meetings of the board on all, or substantially all, matters.
- ◆ It has the right to exercise dominant influence over the undertaking
  - by virtue of provisions contained in the undertaking's Memorandum or Articles
  - by virtue of a control contract. The control contract must be in writing and of a kind authorized by the Memorandum or Articles of the controlled undertaking. It must also be permitted by the law under which that undertaking is established.
- ◆ It is a member of the undertaking and controls alone, pursuant to an agreement with other shareholders or members, a majority of the voting rights in the undertaking.
- ◆ It has the power to exercise, or actually exercises, dominant influence or control over the undertaking.
- ◆ It and the undertaking are managed on a unified basis.

[CA85 s258]

International GAAP

A subsidiary is an entity that is controlled by another. Control is presumed when the parent owns, directly or indirectly, more than 50 per cent of the voting rights, but control can also be deemed to exist in other circumstances:

- ◆ Power over more than half of the voting rights by virtue of an agreement with other investors.
- ◆ Power to govern the financial and operating policies of the entity under a statute or an agreement.
- ◆ Power to appoint or remove the majority of members of the board of directors or equivalent governing body and control of the entity is by that board or body.
- ◆ Power to cast the majority of votes at meetings of the board of directors or equivalent governing body and control of the board or entity is by that board or body.

Comparison

The 2004 UK revisions to the definition of a subsidiary undertaking witnessed the introduction of the term 'power to exercise' into the UK criteria for the first time. This is an anti-avoidance measure to ensure that quasi-subsidiaries cannot escape the consolidation process by claiming that as control has not actually been exercised consolidation is not required.

However, it can be seen that this concept is more ingrained to the definition used by the IASB.

Conversely UK GAAP includes scenarios where control is actually exercised irrespective of the fact that the power to control does not exist. Hence it is possible to classify an entity as a subsidiary under UK GAAP by virtue of dominant influence.

Exemptions from the requirement to produce group accounts

UK GAAP allows exemption from the requirement to produce group financial statements if the group qualifies as a small or medium-sized group and is not ineligible.

Ineligible groups are those that include:

◆ a public company
◆ a company permitted to undertake a regulated activity under the Financial Services and Markets Act 2000
◆ an insurance company.

At the date of publication the size criteria applicable to these designations were as shown in Table 18.1.

Table 18.1 UK size criteria for small and medium groups [CA85 s249(3)]		
	Small	*Medium*
Aggregate net turnover OR	£5.6 million	£22.8 million
Aggregate gross turnover	£6.72 million	£27.36 million
Aggregate net balance sheet total not exceeding OR	£2.8 million	£11.4 million
Aggregate gross balance sheet total not exceeding	£3.36 million	£13.68 million
Average number of employees not exceeding	50	250

Notes

◆ Any two of the three criteria must be applicable.
◆ The terms 'gross' and 'net' refer to the elimination or inclusion of intragroup items.

Similar exemptions for small and medium-sized groups do not exist under international GAAP.

Additionally IAS 27 requires that group accounts are prepared if an entity held subsidiaries at any time during the year, whereas legal rules in the UK only require the preparation of such documents where the parent has subsidiaries at the year-end date.

Excluded subsidiaries

International GAAP does not permit the exclusion of subsidiaries from the consolidation process, although there are some modifications if it can be shown that the entity is 'held for sale'.

UK company legislation does permit exclusion where:

◆ The subsidiary is not material for the purposes of the group accounts giving a true and fair view.

◆ It would be too costly or cause disproportionate delay to collate the information required.

◆ The parent's rights over the subsidiary entity are subject to severe long-term restrictions.

◆ The investment in the subsidiary is held exclusively with a view to resale, and the subsidiary has not previously been consolidated – this prevents creative accounting through the inclusion of subsidiary results when they are favourable and exclusion when poor.

There appears to be a substantial difference between UK and international practice, but this is not the case.

	If a subsidiary is immaterial then by definition it will not impact our view of the consolidated figures.

	FRS 2 does not allow the exclusion of a subsidiary on the grounds of cost or delay, and this overrides the legally permitted exclusion.

	FRS 2 requires, rather than permits, exclusion on the grounds of severe long-term restrictions, but the number of occasions when this occurs is small.

	FRS 2 also requires exclusion on the grounds of held for re-sale, but the 'not previously consolidated' criteria again restricts the frequency when this will be seen.

Non-coterminous year ends

Best accounting practice would indicate that the year end of a subsidiary undertaking should match that of the parent company. However, this will not always be possible, and the question arises of the need for the subsidiary to prepare interim financial statements to facilitate consolidation.

The good news is that subject to certain restrictions the subsidiary can use financial statements prepared to a different reporting date from that of the parent entity.

IAS 27 allows subsidiary financial statements with a year-end date falling within a 3-month window either side of that of the parent to be consolidated. UK GAAP is more restrictive and allows consolidation if the year-end date of the subsidiary falls in the 3 months prior to the parent's year-end date.

Special purpose entities

The key to some of the largest corporate frauds, such as Enron, has been the unscrupulous use of special purpose entities by those involved. These are entities that in substance are controlled by the parent, but legal title has been configured such that this would not be apparent. They can then be used as a method of off-balance-sheet finance holding debt and other obligations that should be disclosed to the stakeholders in the group.

Under UK GAAP these entities are referred to as quasi-subsidiaries by FRS 5 *Reporting the Substance of Transactions*, but do not allow a change of name to confuse your understanding.

Distributions out of pre-acquisition profits

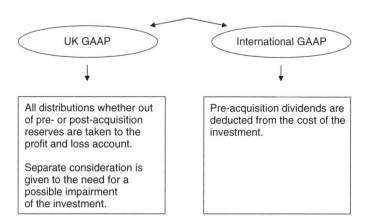

This is a significant difference in accounting practice as by deducting pre-acquisition dividends from the cost they do not get recognized as realized profits and consequently are not available for distribution by the parent.

Disclosure

UK GAAP disclosure requirements are moderately more extensive than those required by IAS 27 due largely to the interaction with the Companies Act 1985.

Box 18.1 Next Group plc (2005) – Details of group companies (UK GAAP)

Group Companies

The Group has taken advantage of Section 231(5) of the Companies Act 1995 in order to list only its principal subsidiary and associated undertaking at 29 January 2005. All these are wholly owned by the Company or its subsidiary undertakings, registered in England and Wales, and operate predominantly in the United Kingdom, unless otherwise stated.

Subsidiary undertakings

NEXT Group Plc	Intermediate holding company
NEXT Retail Limited[1]	Retalling of womenswear, menswear, childrenswear, home products, accessories and fashion jewellery
The NEXT Directory[2]	Home shopping for womenswear, menswear, childrenswear, home products, accessories and fashion jewellery
NEXT Financial Services Limited[1]	Credit card handling and settlement services
Club 24 Limited[1]	Customer and financial services management
Ventura[3]	Customer and financial services management
First Retail Finance Limited[1]	Customer and financial services management
NEXT Sourcing Limited[1]	Overseas sourcing services (Hong Kong)

| NEXT Manufacturing (Pvt) Limited[1] | Garment manufacture (Sri Lanka) |
| NEXT Distribution Limited[1] | Warehousing and distribution services |

Associated undertakings

| Choice Discount Stores Limited[1] | Retailing (40%) |
| Cotton Traders Holdings Limited[1] | Home shopping and retailing (40%) |

[1] Shareholdings held by subsidiary undertakings.
[2] The trade of the NEXT Directory is carried out as a division of NEXT Retail Limited.
[3] Ventura is a trading name of Club 24 Limited.

UK disclosures include:

◆ the name of each group undertaking
◆ if it is incorporated outside Great Britain and its country of incorporation
◆ if unincorporated the address of its principal place of business
◆ whether it is included in the consolidation and, if not, the reasons for exclusion
◆ for each class of shares held, the identity and proportion of the nominal value held of that class.

Box 18.2 Holidaybreak plc (2005) – details of group companies (UK GAAP)

11 Fixed asset investments

	Group		Company	
	2005 £'000	2004 £'000	2005 £'000	2004 £'000
Subsidiary undertakings	–	–	265,145	248,682
Other investments	15	15	–	–
	15	15	265,145	248,682

	Company £'000
Cost and net book value	
At 1 October 2004	248,682
Acquisition of subsidiary undertakings	39,608
Transfer of investments to subsidiary undertakings	(23,145)
At 30 September 2005	265,145

Principal Group investments

The Company and the Group have investments in the following subsidiary undertakings which principally affected the profits and net assets of the Group.

To avoid a statement of excessive length, details of investments which are not significant have been omitted.

All of the subsidiary undertakings have been consolidated in the Group financial statements.

The principal subsidiary undertakings of Holidaybreak plc are as follows:

	Country of incorporation and operation	Proportion of share capital held by the Company (%)	Proportion of share capital held by the Group (%)
Camping operators:			
Greenbank Holidays Limited	England	100	
Easycamp BV	Netherlands		100
Hotel Breaks operators:			

Superbreak Mini-Holidays Limited	England		100
Business Reservations Centre Holland BV	Netherlands		100
Bookit BV	Netherlands		100
BV Weekendjeweg.nl	Netherlands		100
Adventure Travel operators:			
Explore Worldwide Limited	England	100	
Explore Aviation Limited	England		100
Regal Diving & Tours Limited	England	100	
Djoser BV	Netherlands	100	
Holding and other companies:			
Business Reservations Centre Holland Holding BV	Netherlands		100
Eurocamp Travel GmbH	Germany		100
Eurocamp Travel (Schweiz) AG	Switzerland		100
Camping in Comfort BV	Netherlands		100
Keycamp Holidays Netherlands BV	Netherlands		100
Keycamp Holidays (Ireland) Limited	Ireland		100
Eurosites A/S	Denmark		100
Superbreak Mini Holidays Group Limited	England	100	
Eurocamp Travel B.V	Netherlands		100
Camping Division Limited	England	100	
Holidaybreak Air Travel Limited	England	100	

Holidaybreak Trustee Limited	England	100	
Holidaybreak Holding Company Limited	Isle of Man	100	
Holidaybreak Insurance Company Limited	Isle of Man		100
Sites Services SARL	France	100	
Greenbank Packages Limited	England	100	
Greenbank Services Limited	England	100	

Other investments	Group £'000
Cost	
At 1 October 2004 and 30 September 2005	615
Provisions for impairment	
At 1 October 2004 and 30 September 2005	600
Net book value	
At 30 September 2004 and 30 September 2005	15

Other investments (cost of £600,000) are redeemable preference shares in the former printing business of Baldwin Limited. Full provision is retained against this investment.

Do not forget those goodwill differences

The accounting treatment has been examined in detail as part of our consideration of intangible assets, but do not forget that there are some significant differences in accounting practice for purchased goodwill.

◆ UK GAAP requires goodwill to be amortized whereas international practice replaces this procedure with an annual impairment review.

- Negative goodwill (discount on acquisition) is taken directly to the income statement under international GAAP and cannot be capitalized.
- The initial calculation of goodwill under international rules requires the recognition of contingent liabilities.

Main sources of guidance

UK GAAP

- Companies Act 1985
- FRS 2 *Accounting for Subsidiary Undertakings*
- FRS 5 *Reporting the Substance of Transactions.*

International GAAP

- IAS 27 *Consolidated Financial Statements and Accounting for Investments in Subsidiaries*
- IFRS 3 *Business Combinations*
- IFRS 5 *Non-current Assets Held for Sale and Discontinued Operations.*

Key Facts

1. The definition of a subsidiary differs between UK GAAP and international GAAP. The latter focussing on the power to exercise control.

   UK GAAP also includes the actual exercise of control, and this can result in additional entities being classed as subsidiaries through the exercise of dominant influence.

2. Exemption from the requirement to produce group financial statements is available to small and medium-sized groups in the UK – subject to the proviso that they do not contain an ineligible company (e.g. insurance company).

3. When subsidiaries have financial year ends that are non-coterminous with that of the parent company, IAS 27 allows consolidation of financial statements that fall within a 3-month window either side of the parent's year end. UK GAAP is less flexible and only allows this in relation to the 3 months prior to the parent's year-end date.

4. If a subsidiary makes a distribution out of profits earned pre-acquisition, IAS 27 requires these to be deducted from the cost of the investment. This can result in lower distributable reserves as this 'dividend income' is never realized through the income statement.
5. Purchased goodwill is not amortized under international GAAP but is subject to an annual review for impairment.

Group Accounts –
Associates

Setting expectations

An associate represents an investment over which significant influence can be exercised, and have been accounted for using a method known as 'equity accounting' for many years. The underlying methodology of this approach is consistent between UK GAAP and international accounting practice, but there are some differences in the detail, and marked disparities in the way the end result is presented within the financial statements.

Defining an associated undertaking

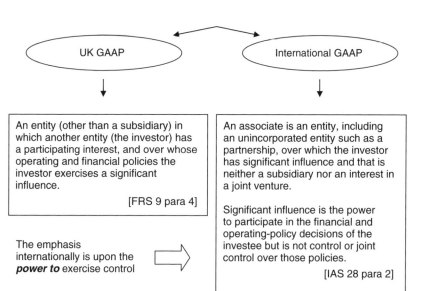

An entity (other than a subsidiary) in which another entity (the investor) has a participating interest, and over whose operating and financial policies the investor exercises a significant influence.

[FRS 9 para 4]

The emphasis internationally is upon the **power to** exercise control

An associate is an entity, including an unincorporated entity such as a partnership, over which the investor has significant influence and that is neither a subsidiary nor an interest in a joint venture.

Significant influence is the power to participate in the financial and operating-policy decisions of the investee but is not control or joint control over those policies.

[IAS 28 para 2]

The use of equity accounting

Under UK GAAP equity accounting is only required in the context of group financial statements, whereas intern. tional GAAP requires a broader application which includes 'economic entity' financial statements. The latter represent the financial statements of an investor that does not have subsidiaries, and consequently are not required to produce consolidated financial statements.

'Economic entity' financial statements should not be confused with 'separate' financial statements. It would be easy to believe that the latter simply represented any financial statements other than consolidated financial statements, but the reality is that the classification is narrower, and effectively restricted to the following circumstances:

◆ An entity required to produce consolidated financial statements additionally produces individual financial statements for the parent company alone. These 'separate' financial statements might be produced voluntarily or be required under local legislation.
◆ Investors specifically exempted from the requirement to consolidate or equity account may produce 'separate' financial statements.

Do not get too concerned about the pedantics of this section, but do remember that unlike UK GAAP equity accounting may be required beyond consolidated financial statements.

The cost method

When 'separate' financial statements are produced an associate is usually recorded using the cost method. As the name implies the associate is recorded at cost in the balance sheet, and the profit and loss account/income statement recognizes distributions from the investee arising after the date of acquisition.

It might appear difficult to create circumstances in which this apparently straightforward approach could differ between UK and international GAAP, but there is one point of disparity. UK GAAP recognizes distributions from the associate within the income statement making no distinction between the payment being made out of pre- or post-acquisition profits. If the investment has been impaired as a result of the distribution this is dealt with separately via an impairment review. Internationally distributions made from pre-acquisition profits represent a reduction in the cost of the investment.

The consequence of the above is that the possibility exists for cost to differ between the two regimes.

Consequences of a poorly performing associate

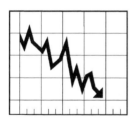

When an investor's share of the losses made by an associate equals or exceeds the value of its interest therein then no further losses should be rocognized unless there is a legal or constructive obligation to do so.

[IAS 28 para 30]

This international rule will look very unfamiliar to those who have grown accustomed to UK GAAP where losses continue to be recognized for as long as there is significant influence.

Presentation

The principle differences in disclosure are centred on the performance statement.

UK GAAP

Box 19.1   BT Group plc (2005) – profit and loss account

	Notes	Before goodwill amortisation and exceptional items £m	Goodwill amortisation and exceptional items £m	Total £m
Total turnover	2	20,182	–	20,182
Group's share of joint ventures' turnover	3	(425)	–	(425)
Group's share of associates' turnover	3	(1,030)	–	(1,030)
Group turnover	2	18,727	–	18,727
Other operating income		215	–	215
Operating costs	4	(16,148)	(218)	(16,366)
Group operating profit (loss)		2,794	(218)	2,576
Group's share of operating profit (loss) of joint ventures	5	(31)	150	119
Group's share of operating profit (loss) of associates	5	212	(2)	210

Total operating profit (loss)		2,975	(70)	2,905
Profit on sale of fixed asset investments	6	–	1,705	1,705
Loss on sale of group undertakings	6	–	(9)	(9)
Profit on sale of property fixed assets		11	–	11
Interest receivable	7	195	–	195
Interest payable	8	(1,341)	(293)	(1,634)
Profit on ordinary activities before taxation		1,840	1,333	3,173
Tax on profit on ordinary activities	9	(598)	139	(459)
Profit on ordinary activities after taxation		1,242	1,472	2,714
Minority interests	10	(5)	(7)	(12)
Profit for the financial year		1,237	1,465	2,702
Dividends	11			(560)
Retained profit for the financial year	25			2,142

Notes

◆ Disclosure of the investor's share of the associate's turnover is not required by UK GAAP but can be given where believed to be helpful to a user of the financial statements. Many large companies did provide this voluntary disclosure.

◆ The investor's share of operating profit must be shown on the face of the profit and loss account.

◆ The investor's share of the associate's interest and tax must also be separately disclosed, but this usually relegated to the note.

Box 19.2   BT Group plc (2005) – Note extracts

8. Interest payable

	2005 £m	2004 £m	2003 £m
Interest payable and similar charges in respect of:			
Bank loans and overdrafts	71	87	82

	2005 £m	2004 £m	2003 £m
Interest payable on finance leases	58	19	–
Other borrowings[ab]	914	1,114	1,527
Group	1,043	1,220	1,609
Joint ventures	23	19	17
Associates	–	–	8
Total interest payable	1,066	1,239	1,634

[a] Includes an exceptional charge of £89 million in the year ended 31 March 2004 being the premium on repurchasing £813 million of the group's issued bonds.

[b] Includes an exceptional charge of £293 million in the year ended 31 March 2003 on the termination of interest rate swap agreements following the receipt of the Cegetel sale proceeds.

9. Tax on Profit (loss) on ordinary activities

	2005 £m	2004 £m	2003 £m
United Kingdom:			
Corporation tax at 30%	542	328	447
Prior year adjustments	4	–	12
Non-UK taxation:			
Current	(4)	37	47
Taxation on the group's share of results of associates and joint ventures	1	–	81
Prior year adjustments	(3)	–	(26)
Total current taxation	540	365	561

International GAAP

IAS 28 *Investments in Associates* requires the consolidated income statement to disclose the investor's share of the associate's profit after taxation. It should be noted that any goodwill-impairment loss relating to the associate for the period would also have been deducted from this figure.

An unusual feature of international disclosure is that although the associate's profit share is post-taxation it is included above the tax line in the income statement proforma.

Box 19.3   BT Group plc (2006) – Income statement

For the year ended 31 March 2006	Notes	Before specific items £m	Specific items £m	Total £m
Revenue	1	19,514	–	19,514
Other operating income	2	227	–	227
Operating costs	3	(17,108)	(138)	(17,246)
Operating profit	1	2,633	(138)	2,495
Finance expense	5	(2,740)	–	(2,740)
Finance income	5	2,268	–	2,268
Net finance expense		(472)	–	(472)
Share of post tax profit of associates and joint ventures	16	16	–	16
Profit on disposal of joint venture		–	1	1
Profit before taxation		2,177	(137)	2,040
Taxation	6	(533)	41	(492)
Profit for the year		1,644	(96)	1,548

Main sources of guidance

UK GAAP

♦ Companies Act 1985
♦ FRS 9 *Associates and Joint Ventures.*

International Accounting Standards

208

International GAAP

◆ IAS 28 *Investments in Associates.*

Key facts

1. The benchmark for associate accounting remains equity accounting but there are some differences in application and disclosure.
2. Unlike UK GAAP there are occasions when IAS 28 requires equity accounting to be used outside the scope of consolidated financial statements.
3. Unless there is a contractual obligation IAS 28 requires the recognition of associate losses to cease when they exceed the value of the investment. Under UK GAAP the investor would continue to recognize their share of these losses.
4. International GAAP restricts mandatory income statement disclosure relating to associates to a single figure, namely the investor's share of the associate's profit after taxation less any impairment losses for the period.

Group Accounts – Joint
Ventures

Setting expectations

FRS 9 *Associates and Joint Ventures* recognizes two types of joint arrangement.

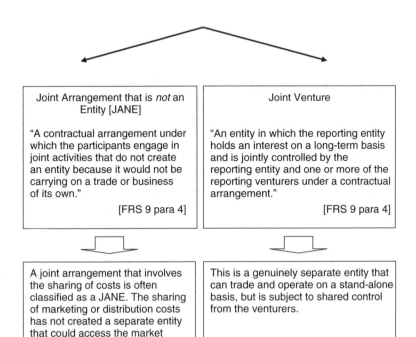

IAS 31 *Interests in Joint Ventures* recognizes three categories of joint arrangement.

1. *Jointly controlled operations*

A well-documented example of such an arrangement is when several entities collaborate in the construction of an aircraft.

One venturer might produce the engines, another the internal fittings and so on. In UK terms this would equate to a JANE as each participant uses their own assets and incurs their own costs; there is no separate entity that could stand-alone and trade independently.

Each entity will record its own costs, whilst shared costs and proceeds from the sale of the aircraft will be split under the terms of the contractual arrangement agreed at the outset.

2. *Jointly controlled assets*

This is when two or more venturers share the cost of constructing an asset that will benefit and be used by all of them. An oil pipeline used to transport crude oil from a distant oilfield might be shared by several companies as the cost of building a unique pipeline for each individual company would be prohibitive.

The accounting treatment would again be similar to a JANE with each venturer taking an agreed share of the cost to their own financial statements.

3. *Jointly controlled entity*

As implied by the name this is a discrete entity that operates independently but is controlled by two or more other parties. As with the joint venture described for UK GAAP this requires the preparation of its own financial statements that then have to be combined with those of the investors to reflect the control they exercise over its financial and operating decisions.

Accounting for a joint venture

JANEs or their international equivalents cause few accounting difficulties although it should be noted that some interests accounted for as a JANE under UK GAAP may be defined as a jointly controlled entity by IAS 31. This divergence arises because IAS 31 places a heavy emphasis upon the existence of a legally separate entity, whilst FRS 9 asks if a separate entity exists in substance.

If the existence of a joint venture/jointly controlled entity is established FRS 9 requires the use of gross equity accounting in the preparation of the consolidated financial statements. The technique used is identical to that used for associates but some additional disclosures are required.

Internationally the preparers of group financial statements have a choice of methodology between equity accounting and proportional consolidation, although it is made clear that the latter is the preferred option. The method selected will have a pronounced impact on the figures reported and any quantitative analysis performed. Let us consider the two methods in snapshot.

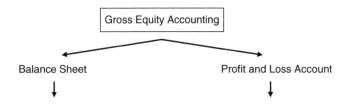

| | | Balance Sheet | | Profit and Loss Account | |

The investment in the joint venture is shown as adjacent lines within fixed assets.

Line 1: The investor's share of the fair value of the joint venturer's assets including any unamortized goodwill.

Line 2: The investor's share of the fair value of the joint venturer's liabilities.

The investor's share to be disclosed of the following:

• Turnover
• Operating profit
• Exceptionals
• Interest
• Tax

As with associates the separate disclosure of interest and tax is often relegated to the notes.

Box 20.1   Tesco plc (2004) – Balance sheet extract

					Group	Company	
	note	£m	2004 £m	£m	2003 £m	2004 £m	2003 £m
Fixed assets							
Intangible assets	12		965		890	–	–
Tangible assets	13		14,094		12,828	–	–
Investments	14		34		59	9,077	7,820
Investments in joint ventures	14						
Share of gross assets		2,006		1,708		–	–
Less share of gross liabilities		(1,712)		(1,459)		–	–
Goodwill		15		17		–	–
			309		266	143	158
Investments in associates	14		21		18	–	
			15,423		14,061	9,220	7,978

This reflects the presentation of a joint venture under UK GAAP using the gross equity method.

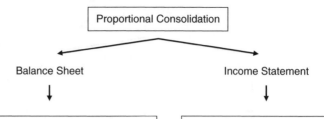

Balance Sheet	Income Statement
The investment in the jointly controlled entity is accounted for by combining the venturers own balance sheet with its share of the fair value of assets and liabilities of its investment on a line-by-line basis. As with equity accounting no minority interest will arise.	As with the balance sheet a line-by-line aggregation is performed, bringing in the venturer's share of revenue and costs.

Box 20.2   Tate & Lyle plc (2006) – Accounting policy extract

2 Group accounting policies

Basis of consolidation

(a) Subsidiaries

Subsidiaries are all entities over which the Group has the power to govern the financial and operating policies, generally accompanying a shareholding of more than one half of the voting rights and taking into account the existence of potential voting rights. Subsidiaries are fully consolidated from the date on which control is transferred to the Group. They are de-consolidated from the data that control ceases. The purchase method of accounting is used to account for the acquisition of subsidiaries by the Group. The recognised identifiable assets, liabilities and contingent liabilities of a subsidiary are measured at their fair values at the date of acquisition. The interest of minority shareholders is stated at the minority's proportion of the fair values of the identifiable assets, liabilities and contingent liabilities recognised. Where necessary, adjustments are made to the financial statements of subsidiaries to bring the accounting policies used into line with those used by the Group. All inter-company transactions and balances between Group entities are eliminated on consolidation.

(b) Joint ventures

An entity is regarded as a joint venture if the Group has joint control over its operating and financial policies. The Group's interests in jointly controlled entities are accounted for by proportionate consolidation, whereby the Group's share of the joint ventures' income and expenses, assets and liabilities and cash flows are combined on a line-by-line basis with similar items in the Group's financial statements. Where necessary adjustments are made to the financial statements of joint ventures to bring the accounting policies used into line with those used by the Group. The Group recognises the position of gains or losses on the sale of assets to the joint venture that is attributable to the other ventures. The Group does not recognise its share of profits or losses from the joint venture that result from the Group's purchase of assets from the joint venture until it resells the assets to an external entity.

(c) Associates

An entity is regarded as an associate if the Group has significant influence, but not control, over its operating and financial policies. Significant influence generally exists where the Group holds more than 20% and less than 50% of the shareholders' voting rights. Associates are accounted for under the equity method whereby the Group's income statement includes its share of their profits and losses and the Group's balance sheet includes its share of their net assets. Where necessary, adjustments are made to the financial statements of associates to bring the accounting policies used into line with those used by the Group. When the Group's share of losses in an associate equals or exceeds its interest in the associate, including any other unsecured receivables, the Group does not recognise further losses, unless it has incurred obligations or made payments on behalf of the associate.

Déjà vu

Several of the differences between UK and international GAAP described for associates recur when considering joint ventures.

◆ Equity accounting or proportional consolidation can sometimes be required in separate financial statements. This differs from UK

GAAP where the use of these methods is restricted to consolidated financial statements.

- Losses on a jointly controlled entity are recognized under IAS 31 only until the value of the investors interest has been reduced to nil (i.e. it cannot go negative).

   UK GAAP continues to recognize losses until joint control ceases.

- International GAAP requires dividends paid out of pre-acquisition profits to be treated as a deduction from cost, whereas the UK approach is to recognize pre- and post-acquisition dividends within the profit and loss account, and then perform a separate impairment review of the investment.

Main sources of guidance

UK GAAP

- Companies Act 1985
- FRS 9 *Associates and Joint Ventures.*

International GAAP

- IAS 31 *Interests in Joint Ventures.*

Key Facts

1. Few accounting problems arise from JANEs (Joint Arrangement Not an Entity), and their international equivalents, jointly controlled assets and operations, as these are normally associated with the allocation of costs but there is no stand-alone entity over which control is exercised.
2. UK GAAP accounts for joint ventures, where control of a separate entity is shared between two or more venturers, using gross equity accounting.
3. Internationally a choice of accounting treatment exists for jointly controlled entities. The preferred option is proportional consolidation but equity accounting is also permitted.

Group Accounts – Merger Accounting: The End of the Road

Setting expectations

One of the goals of a universal accounting rule set is to reduce choice and thereby facilitate the review of financial information. Towards this end the days of merger accounting appear to be numbered with IFRS 3 *Business Combinations* banning this method so that acquisition accounting becomes the only acceptable approach.

UK GAAP remains the last bastion of merger accounting although the ASB has indicated that it will eventually be prohibited when the latest phase of the IASB's work on business combinations is complete and subsequently adopted in the UK.

For the reasons outlined above it is not the aim of this text to look at every aspect of merger accounting, but as it remains a viable, if rare, method available to UK companies not adopting international GAAP a resume is given of the main features.

When can merger accounting be used in the UK?

Merger accounting cannot be used unless a series of criteria set out by the Companies Act 1985 and FRS 6 *Acquisitions and Mergers* are met in full, whereupon it becomes mandatory.

Companies Act 1985 criteria

- ◆ After the combination at least 90 per cent of the nominal value of shares carrying unrestricted rights to participate in distributions are held by or on behalf of the parent or its subsidiaries.
- ◆ The holding was acquired via an arrangement providing for the issue of equity shares by a parent or its subsidiaries.
- ◆ The fair value of any consideration other than the issue of equity shares is not more than 10 per cent of the nominal value of the equity shares issued.
- ◆ Adoption of the merger method of accounting accords with UK GAAP (i.e. FRS 6).

FRS 6 (para 6–11) criteria

- ◆ No party to the combination is portrayed as acquirer or acquiree.

- ◆ All parties to the combination participate in establishing the management structure and decisions are made by consensus.
- ◆ Relative sizes are not so disparate that one entity dominates the other by virtue of size. A party would be presumed to dominate if more than 50 per cent larger than the other.
- ◆ The consideration given must meet the following requirements:
  - – Consideration for equity shares obtained comprises primarily equity shares in the combined entity
  - – Any non-equity consideration is an immaterial proportion of the fair value of the consideration
  - – Take into account consideration for equity shares acquired in the 2 years prior to the combination.
- ◆ No equity shareholders retain any material interest in the future performance of only part of the combined entity.

Key differences compared to acquisition accounting

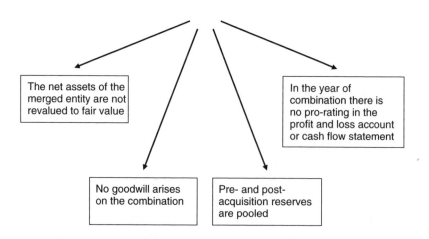

These differences potentially make merger accounting an attractive method. The low asset values result in a lower depreciation expense, and this coupled with a full year's profit in the year of combination make profits higher. Simultaneously asset values are lower and hence a favourable return on capital employed results from these two effects.

Main sources of guidance

UK GAAP

- Companies Act 1985
- FRS 6 *Acquisitions and Mergers*.

International GAAP

- IFRS 3 *Business Combinations*.

Key Facts

1. An awareness of merger accounting principles is useful as the method is allowed under existing UK GAAP. However, it will be banned in the future bringing consistency of treatment with international GAAP, which allows only acquisition accounting.

Narrowing the Divide – UK GAAP Goes International

Setting expectations

The enforced adoption of international accounting standards by UK listed companies that produce consolidated financial statements, and the encouragement given to other entities to voluntarily move to this rule set means that UK GAAP and its proponents have a choice – evolve or fade away. The ASB (Accounting Standards Board) have taken a proactive approach and been heavily involved in the development of IFRS with a view that subject to certain safeguards existing UK accounting standards will gradually be replaced by their international counterparts. Blanket adoption without modification is not an option for a variety of reasons including:

◆ Inconsistencies with national legislation need to be eliminated.
◆ Additional disclosures maybe considered appropriate to the UK market.
◆ Many small companies in the UK use the FRSSE (Financial Reporting Standard for Smaller Entities) for the preparation of their financial statements for which there is currently no direct international equivalent.

However, UK and international accounting standards are gradually becoming unified and the following UK standards are effectively the international equivalent rebadged upon approval for UK adoption by the ASB.

UK Standard	International Standard	
FRS 20	IFRS 2	Share-based Payment
FRS 21	IAS 10	Events after the Balance-Sheet Date
FRS 22	IAS 33	Earnings Per Share
FRS 23	IAS 21	The Effects of Changes in Foreign Exchange Rates
FRS 24	IAS 29	Financial Reporting in Hyperinflationary Economies
FRS 25	IAS 32	Financial Instruments: Disclosure and Presentation
FRS 26	IAS 39	Financial Instruments: Measurement
FRS 27	See Note 1	Life Assurance
FRS 28	See Note 2	Corresponding Amounts
FRS 29	IFRS 7	Financial Instruments: Disclosures

Note 1: The ASB reached an agreement with the Association of British Insurers and the major UK life assurers in the form of a Memorandum of Understanding for the implementation of this standard. Under the terms of this agreement the life assurance industry has agreed to implement this standard even though as entities reporting under IFRS it would not be mandatory for them to do so.

Note 2: The ASB considered adopting the international rules on corresponding amounts, but decided against this approach as international guidance is contained in several standards and it was seen as inappropriate that sections of international standards be introduced on a piecemeal basis.

Just for the record the international standards involved would be:

◆ IAS 1 *Presentation of Financial Statements*
◆ IAS 8 *Accounting Policies, Changes in Accounting Estimates and Errors*
◆ IFRS 1 *First-Time Adoption of International Financial Reporting Standards*

Upon first examination the subjects covered by accounting standards that have been unified between UK and international GAAP would seem beyond the scope of this text, the primary purpose of which is to help you understand the differences and the consequential adjustments needed to move from one to another. However, FRS 20 was issued in 2004, and hence the time span covered by this and subsequent standards since their implementation has been modest, and so a brief snapshot will be given of the changes that were introduced with the international rules.

Share-based payment

Prior to the adoption of IFRS 2 *Share-based Payment* there was no accounting standard in the UK dealing with this subject. The application of FRS 20 was required for accounting periods starting on or after 1 January 2005 although unlisted entities were given an additional year.

Technically many parties can be remunerated for their goods or services in the form of share capital or options giving rights to shares in the future. However, the real impact centred upon the remuneration of staff, and the introduction of FRS 20 was greeted in some quarters with portents of doom for reported profits – in some instances this had justification. To understand the repercussions of this standard we need to examine the accounting environment prior to its introduction.

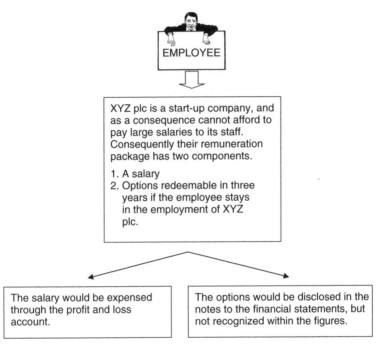

FRS 20/IFRS 2 require the 'cost' of providing the options to be recognized as an expense – a move that proved very unpopular with the high technology sector where options were commonly awarded to staff as an incentive for them to continue in employment with the issuer. Clearly the employee is also accepting an element of risk as at the vesting date of the options the share price might be below the strike price of the options effectively rendering them worthless.

The standard identifies two distinct types of share-based payment.

1. Equity settled (Example 22.1)
2. Cash settled (Example 22.2).

In both cases the concept that no direct cost implies there should be no charge against profits is dispelled.

Example 22.1

Equity-settled share-based payment

A company grants 1,000 share options to each of its twenty employees on 1 July 2003. Each grant is conditional upon the employee remaining in employment with the company for the next 4 years. At the grant date the fair value of an option is calculated at £12.

The workforce has always been very loyal to the company and it is anticipated that eighteen will remain in employment at the end of the 4-year term.

Unfortunately the estimate relating to the number of employees proves to be inaccurate, with four staff leaving in year 1 and a further member of staff resigning in each of the following 2 years. Each resignation was not anticipated by the finance director preparing the figures for inclusion in the financial statements.

What expense should the company recognize in each year ended 30 June over the term of the option?

Year ended 30 June 2004

$$\text{Expense} = 1{,}000 \text{ options} \times £12 \times \frac{16}{20} \times \frac{1}{4} \text{ years} = \textbf{£2400}$$

Year ended 30 June 2005

$$\text{Expense} = 1{,}000 \text{ options} \times £12 \times \frac{15}{20} \times \frac{2}{4} \text{ years} = £4{,}500$$

But £2,400 already recognized in 2004

Hence 2005 expense = **£2,100**

Year ended 30 June 2006

$$\text{Expense} = 1{,}000 \text{ options} \times £12 \times \frac{14}{20} \times \frac{3}{4} \text{ years} = £6{,}300$$

But £4,500 already recognized in 2004/05

Hence 2005 expense = **£1,800**

Year ended 30 June 2007

Expense $= 1{,}000$ options $\times £12 \times \dfrac{14}{20} \times \dfrac{4}{4}$ years $= £8{,}400$

But £6,300 already recognized in 2004/05/06

Hence 2005 expense $= £2{,}100$

Note that for equity-settled share-based payment the fair value of the option at the grant date is used throughout the vesting period.

Box 22.1   Topps Tiles plc (2006) – Accounting policy note extract

s) Share-based payments

The Group has applied the requirements of IFRS 2 Share-based Payments. In accordance with the transitional provisions, IFRS 2 will be applied to all grants of equity instruments after 7 November 2002 that were unvested as of 1 January 2005.

The Group issues equity settled share based payments to certain employees. Equity settled share based payments are measured at fair value at the date of grant. The fair value determined at the grant date of the share based payment is expensed on a straight line basis over the vesting period, based on the Group's estimate of shares that will eventually vest. Fair value is measured by use of the Black Scholes model.

The Group provides employees with the ability to purchase the Group's ordinary shares at 80 per cent of the current market value through the operation of it's share save scheme. The Group records an expense, based on its estimate of the 20 per cent discount related to shares expected to vest on a straight line basis over the vesting period.

By contrast cash-settled equity-based payment adjusts the fair value of the option at the end of each accounting period. A good example of cash-settled equity share-based payment is provided by SARs (Share Appreciation Rights).

SARs: A right to receive a bonus equal to the appreciation in the companies share price over a specified period.

Example 22.2

Cash-settled equity-based payment

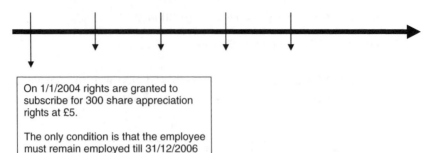

On 1/1/2004 rights are granted to
subscribe for 300 share appreciation
rights at £5.

The only condition is that the employee
must remain employed till 31/12/2006

Share prices and FV of the options on the last day of the year are as
follows:

Year	Share Price [£]	FV of Option
2004	4	50p
2005	6	60p
2006	8	70p

The employee stays employed and decides to exercise the option on
31/12/2004.

What is the impact on the profit and loss account in the years 2004
to 2006?

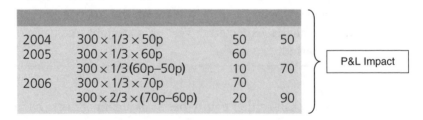

2004	$300 \times 1/3 \times 50p$	50	50
2005	$300 \times 1/3 \times 60p$	60	
	$300 \times 1/3 (60p-50p)$	10	70
2006	$300 \times 1/3 \times 70p$	70	
	$300 \times 2/3 \times (70p-60p)$	20	90

P&L Impact

Events after the balance-sheet date

For accounting periods beginning on or after 1 January 2005 all UK
companies, with the exception of those using the FRSSE (Financial Reporting Standard for Smaller Entities), have been required

to comply with FRS 21 *Events after the Balance-Sheet Date.* This standard is a mirror of the international equivalent on this subject, but prior to this date there were some key differences in approach.

To fully appreciate these earlier differences it should be remembered that two categories of post-balance sheet can be identified with one of these capable of further division.

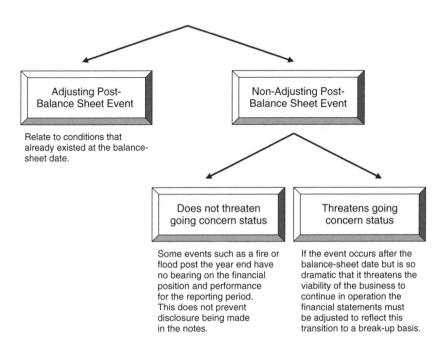

The most significant change occurring in the transition from the old to the new rules related to the recognition of dividends. Prior to 2005 final dividends declared after the financial year end were still recognized in the financial statements whereas the new rules require recognition to be made in the financial period when the declaration is made. For some companies this resulted in an apparent dramatic increase to reserves.

Box 22.2   AstraZeneca plc (2005) – UK GAAP to IFRS reconciliation (extract)

Total equity	31 Dec 2004 $m
Total equity under UK GAAP	14,519
Adjustments to conform to IFRS	
Employee benefits	(2,010)
Financial Instruments	11
Share-based payments	–
Goodwill	108
Dividends	1,061
Capitalised software and other Intangibles	106
Other	12
Deferred tax – IFRS adjustments above	579
– Other	111
Total equity under IFRS	**14,497**

The explanation for this adjustment can be easily seen if we examine a time-line of events.

Example 22.3

The transition to new IFRS rules – Dividends

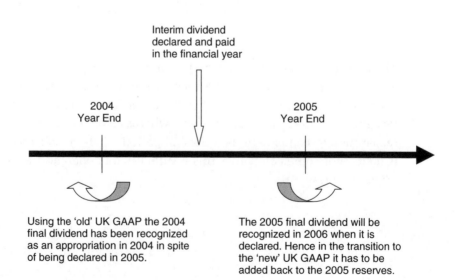

Interim dividend declared and paid in the financial year

2004 Year End

2005 Year End

Using the 'old' UK GAAP the 2004 final dividend has been recognized as an appropriation in 2004 in spite of being declared in 2005.

The 2005 final dividend will be recognized in 2006 when it is declared. Hence in the transition to the 'new' UK GAAP it has to be added back to the 2005 reserves.

Earnings per share

With the introduction of FRS 22 *Earnings Per Share* UK GAAP became synonymous with international practice, although as with all such adoptions companies using the FRSSE were exempted due to the current lack of international guidance bespoke to small entities. The previous UK standard (FRS 14 *Earnings per Share*) did not differ markedly from current practice, and with the exception of very minor technical disparities the differences lie within the disclosure to be given.

◆ If additional EPS figures are provided (i.e. beyond basic and diluted EPS) international GAAP does not require the reason to be given, but if the earnings do not correspond to a line in the profit and loss account a reconciliation must be provided.

◆ When calculating diluted EPS each diluting factor has to be considered separately and anti-dilutive securities excluded from the calculation. Prior to the introduction of international rules the disclosure of anti-dilutive securities was not required.

Box 2.23 Greggs plc (2005) – Income statement and note extracts showing typical EPS disclosures

Consolidated Income Statement
for the 52 weeks ended 31 December 2005
(2004: 53 weeks ended 1 January 2005)

	Note	2005 £'000	2004 £'000
Revenue	1	533,435	504,186
Cost of sales	2	(203,346)	(192,860)
Gross profit		330,089	311,326
Distribution and selling costs	2	(247,188)	(229,510)
Administrative expenses	2	(35,758)	(36,053)
Operating profit		47,143	45,763
Finance income	5	3,106	2,003
Finance expenses	6	(90)	(15)
Profit before tax	3–4	50,159	47,751
Income tax	8	(16,085)	(15,474)
Profit for the financial year attributable to equity holders of the parent		34,074	32,277
Basic earnings per share	9	282.1p	270.5p
Diluted earnings per share	9	278.9p	267.7p

9. Earnings per share

Basic earnings per share

The calculation of basic earnings per share for the year ended 31 December 2005 was based on profit attributable to ordinary shareholders of £34,074,000 (2004: £32,277,000)and a weighted average number of ordinary shares outstanding during the year ended 31 December 2005 of 12,080,526 (2004: 11,931,728), calculated as follows:

Weighted average number of ordinary shares

	2005 Number	2004 Number
Issued ordinary shares at start of year	12,141,892	12,109,483
Effect of own shares held	(79,333)	(195,196)
Effect of shares issued	17,967	17,441
Weighted average number of ordinary shares during the year	12,080,526	11,931,728

Diluted earnings per share

The calculation of diluted earnings per share for the year ended 31 December 2005 was based on profit attributable to ordinary shareholders of £34,074,000 (2004: £32,277,000) and a weighted average number of ordinary shares outstanding during the year ended 31 December 2005 of 12,215,800 (2004: 12,055,134), calculated as follows:

Weighted average number of ordinary shares (diluted)

	2005 Number	2004 Number
Weighted average number of ordinary shares during the year	12,080,526	11,931,728
Effect of share options on issue	135,274	123,406
Weighted average number of ordinary shares (diluted) during the year	12,215,800	12,055,134

Foreign currency translation

Prior to the alignment with international practice the accounting treatment for foreign currency translation was encapsulated within SSAP 20 *Foreign Currency Translation*. There were a number of key differences between old and new practice.

Key difference 1: Currency concepts

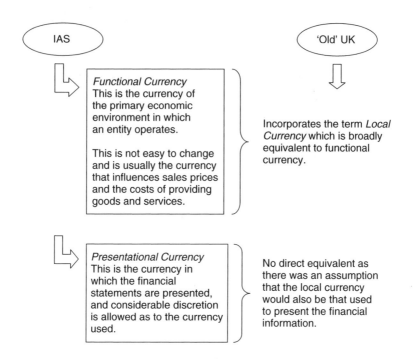

IAS

'Old' UK

Functional Currency
This is the currency of the primary economic environment in which an entity operates.

This is not easy to change and is usually the currency that influences sales prices and the costs of providing goods and services.

Incorporates the term *Local Currency* which is broadly equivalent to functional currency.

Presentational Currency
This is the currency in which the financial statements are presented, and considerable discretion is allowed as to the currency used.

No direct equivalent as there was an assumption that the local currency would also be that used to present the financial information.

Key difference 2: Goodbye choice

As part of the consolidation process for an international group the financial statements of overseas entities need to be converted into a common currency to that of the parent. Prior to adoption of international rules UK GAAP described two potential methods by which to achieve this objective. The selection of method was determined by the autonomy of the overseas operation.

Temporal method

The overseas entity is heavily dependent on the parent. This could be evidenced by regular cash flows between the two entities.

Non-monetary assets in the balance sheet of the overseas entity (i.e. fixed assets and stock) would be translated at the historic rate of exchange applying at their acquisition whereas monetary assets where translated at the closing rate.

Closing Rate method

The overseas entity operates autonomously making its own financial and operating decisions. Cash flows between the entities would be restricted to intermittent transactions such as the payment of a dividend.

The balance sheet of the overseas entity was translated using the closing rate. Foreign exchange movements were taken directly to the reserves.

IAS 21 (i.e. FRS 23) does not have a choice as there is no direct equivalent to the temporal method. However, it should be noted that an overseas entity that is non-autonomous relying on the parent for guidance on its operating and financing decisions is likely to have the same functional currency as the parent.

It should also be noted that when translating the profit and loss account of the overseas entity under the closing rate method it was permitted to use the average or closing exchange rate providing this was done consistently. International practice, as now adopted through FRS 22, does not allow this choice with only the average rate being permitted.

The method now used by UK entities, usually referred to as the net investment method, is excellently summarized by their accounting policies.

Box 22.4   Amstrad plc (2005) – Accounting policy extract

(j) **Foreign currencies** (continued)

   (iii) **Overseas subsidiary**

      The balance sheet of the Group's overseas subsidiary is translated into Sterling at the rate of exchange ruling at the balance sheet date. The results of the overseas subsidiary are translated into Sterling at average month end rates. The difference between the income statement of the foreign subsidiary translated at the average exchange rate and the closing exchange rate is recorded as part of the Group's translation reserve.

Exchange differences arising on the translation of the opening net assets of the overseas subsidiary are also recorded as part of the Group's translation reserve. When a foreign subsidiary is sold, such exchange differences are recognised in the income statement as part of the gain or loss on sale.

Key difference 3: Recycling

The concept of recycling had been largely eliminated from UK GAAP prior to the decision to adopt international accounting practice, and hence was not a feature of SSAP 20. Under FRS 22 foreign exchange gains or losses taken to the reserves as required by the net investment method are recycled through the profit and loss account upon the disposal of the overseas entity. This is achieved by adjusting the gain or loss on disposal.

Key difference 4: Goodwill is an asset

International practice understandably views goodwill arising from an acquisition as an asset, and consistently with other assets and liabilities translates it at the closing rate. This results in an exchange gain or loss being created on the goodwill balance which is recognized in reserves in common with other exchange movements arising under the net investment method. This contrasts with 'old' UK practice where no foreign exchange movement was recognized on goodwill.

Key difference 5: Other differences of note

◆ International rules do not allow a transaction to be reported using a contracted rate (i.e. restricted to actual rate or average rate).
◆ Foreign exchange movements represent a risk that many entities will try to mitigate by the use of hedging. However, under international best practice all guidance on hedge accounting has been removed from IAS 21 (FRS 22), and is now covered by accounting standards dealing with financial instruments.

Box 22.5 Amstrad plc (2005/06) – Consolidation statement of changes in equity

25. Consolidated statement of changes in equity

	Called up Share Capital £000	Share Premium Account £000	Share Option Reserve £000	Translation Reserve £000	Capital Reserve £000	Retained Earnings £000	Total £000
Balance at 1 July 2005 pre IAS39 adjustment	8,166	6,593	74	43	3,618	27,485	45,979
IAS39 adjustment	–	–	–	–	–	570	570
Revised balance at 1 July 2005	8,166	6,593	74	43	3,618	28,055	46,549
Profit for the financial year	–	–	–	–	–	15,089	15,089
Recognised directly in equity:							
Dividends	–	–	–	–	–	(5,760)	(5,76)
Exercise of equity share options	124	295	–	–	–	–	419
Provision for share based payments	–	–	79	–	–	–	79
Currency translation differences on foreign currency net investments	–	–	–	(74)	–	–	(74)
Balance at 30 June 2006	8,290	6,888	153	(31)	3,618	37,384	56,302

The share premium account records the consideration premium for shares issued at a value that exceeds their nominal value.
The share option reserve represents the fair value of share options granted as outlined in note 24.
The translation reserve is used to record exchange differences arising from translation of the financial statements of the Group's overseas subsidiary.
The capital reserve arose in 1999 and 2000 in relation to corporate restructuring.

Hyperinflationary economies

The definition of hyperinflation given by IAS 29 *Financial Reporting in Hyperinflationary Economies* provides clear guidance on what characterizes this phenomenon:

♦ The general population prefers to keep its wealth in non-monetary assets or in a relatively stable foreign currency. Amounts of local currency held are immediately invested to maintain purchasing power.
♦ The general population regards monetary amounts not in terms of local currency but in terms of a relatively stable foreign currency – prices may be quoted in that currency.
♦ Sales and purchases on credit take place at prices that compensate for the expected loss of purchasing power during the credit period, even if the period is short.
♦ Interest rates, wages and prices are linked to a price index.
♦ The cumulative inflation rate over 3 years approaches, or exceeds, 100 per cent.

[IAS 29 para 3]

Unlike 'old' UK practice that allowed two possible approaches to adjusting for hyperinflation this has now been restricted to a single method. The balance sheet being adjusted for movements in a general price index thereby avoiding the problem of fixed assets effectively being 'lost' from the consolidated financial statements as their translated value is eroded by inflation.

Financial instruments

As the capital markets have evolved so increasingly complex financial instruments have been developed to service a growing appetite for inventive financing strategies. Without comprehensive accounting guidance on tackling these instruments the potential for misleading, intentionally or otherwise, a reader of the financial statements is considerable.

The task for those leading the accounting profession was immense, and could be subdivided into two categories:

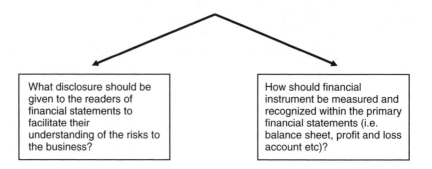

The first step taken in the UK took the form of FRS 13 *Derivatives and Other Financial Instruments: Disclosures* issued in 1998. This reflected a pragmatic view by the ASB who recognized that the problems associated with measuring financial instruments were both difficult and contentious, and that waiting for these to be resolved would lead to a prolonged period of no guidance. At least if companies were required to give extensive disclosures this would help stakeholders to make an informed decision.

However many of the problems associated with lack of recognition continued.

◆ The value of financial instruments often varies widely over the period to their maturity leading to unrealized gains and losses of which the reader is unaware until the maturity date when the crystallization of the gain or loss would come as something of a surprise.

Example 22.4

The unseen dangers of a forward contract

The seller contracts to sell 1,000 tonnes of coffee beans to the buyer for £500 per tonne in 6 months. The contract is signed on 1 October 2006, and the seller's financial year end is 31 December.

BUYER   SELLER

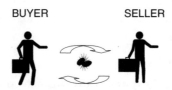

During the 6-month term of the contract commodity prices move to reflect the pressures of supply and demand. The prices on key dates are as follows:

31 December 2006	£650 per tonne
31 March 2007-01-27	£750 per tonne

If the underlying price movements are not incorporated in the financial statements the readers of the 2007 financial statements produced by the seller might be in for a nasty shock. On this contract alone the seller is obligated to go to the commodity market and buy 1,000 tonnes of coffee beans on 31 March 2007 to service the contract. These will be purchased at £750 per tonne, but will be sold to the buyer at the contracted rate of £500 per tonne. A loss of £250,000 (i.e. 1,000 tonnes × £250) is realized.

By contrast if the open position on the contract had been measured at the 2006 year end a loss of £150,000 would have been recognized at that date. This would give a reader of the accounts an early warning of the potential losses on the contract (remember commodity prices could move in the opposite direction before maturity), and match the losses to the period when they have effectively been incurred.

> NOTE: In reality for the majority of such contracts the coffee beans are neither required by the buyer nor the seller as the contract will be settled in cash on the maturity date for the amount of the gain or loss realized.

The challenges of producing accounting guidance for the measurement of all financial instruments were immense, and it was inevitable that whatever recommendations were made they would be the subject of fierce criticism. Undaunted the IASB has now issued three accounting standards dealing with all aspects of financial instruments including IAS 39 dealing with their recognition and measurement. This is probably the most extensive and complex accounting standard that has come to fruition and even its implementation has not been without pitfalls.

◆ The EU excluded certain sections for entities listed within its boundaries. These exclusions were known as the EU carve-outs.

◆ In the UK the release of financial reporting standards to mirror their international counterparts encountered timing difficulties leading to the implementation of large sections being delayed.

The purpose of this text is not to examine in detail the accounting approach adopted for financial instruments, but here are a few of the highlights.

◆ Although many financial instruments, particularly derivatives, are very complex in nature the definition of this term is very broad.

> A financial instrument is any contract that gives rise to a financial asset of one entity and a financial liability or equity instrument of another entity.

It is important to realize that the scope of this definition includes trade receivables, bank loans, equity share capital and so on.

◆ Financial assets are sub-divided into four categories.

Financial assets at fair value through profit or loss	◆ Any asset so designated on initial recognition [irrevocable] ◆ Assets held for trading ◆ Derivatives unless accounted for as part of a cash flow hedge or a net investment hedge
Loans and receivables	◆ Non-derivative financial assets with fixed or determinable payments that are not quoted on an active market
Held-to-maturity investments	◆ Financial assets with fixed or determinable payments and fixed maturity that the entity has the *positive intent and ability* to hold to maturity [i.e. indifferent to profit opportunities arising from changes in the fair value]
Available-for-sale	◆ Assets not classified in any of the other categories ◆ Assets so designated on initial recognition [often assets held for liquidity purposes]

Different categories of asset are subject to differing accounting treatments.

Financial assets at fair value through profit or loss	These are marked to fair value and the movements taken direct to the profit and loss account
Loans and receivables	Initially recorded at fair value and then accounted for using amortized cost
Held-to-maturity investments	Initially recorded at fair value and then accounted for using amortized cost
Available-for-sale	These are remeasured to their fair value but the movements are taken directly to the reserves. However if the asset is sold or subject to an impairment the gains and losses taken to reserves are recycled through the face of the profit and loss account.

A reminder of the accounting treatment can usually be found within the accounting policies note of the entity being reviewed.

Box 22.6 BT Group plc (2006) – Accounting policy note extract

(XX) FINANCIAL INSTRUMENTS (FROM 1 APRIL 2005)

The following are the key accounting policies used in the preparation of the restated 1 April 2005 opening balance sheet and subsequent periods to reflect the adoption of IAS 32, 'Financial Instruments: Disclosure and Presentation' and IAS 39, 'Financial Instruments: Recognition and Measurement'.

Financial assets

Purchases and sales of financial assets

All regular way purchases and sales of financial assets are recognized on the settlement date, which is the date that the asset is delivered to or by the group.

Financial assets at fair value through income statement

A financial asset is classified in this category if acquired principally for the purpose of selling in the short term or if so designated by management. Financial assets held in this category are initially recognized and subsequently measured at fair value, with changes in value recognised in the income statement in the line which most appropriately reflects the nature of the item or transaction.

Loans and receivables

Loans and receivables are non-derivative financial assets with fixed or determinable payments that are not quoted in an active market other than:

◆ those that the group intends to sell immediately or in the short term, which are classified as held for trading;
◆ those for which the group may not recover substantially all of its initial investment, other than because of credit deterioration, which are classified as available for sale.

Loans and receivables are initially recognized at fair value plus transaction costs and subsequently carried at amortised cost using the effective interest method, with changes in carrying value recognised in the income statement in the line which most appropriately reflects the nature of the item or transaction.

Available-for-sale financial assets

Non-derivative financial assets classified as available-for-sale are either specifically designated in this category or not classified in any of the other categories. Available-for-sale financial assets are carried at fair value, with unrealised gains and losses (except for changes in exchange rates for monetary items, interest, dividends and impairment losses which are recognised in the income statement) are recognised in equity until the financial asset is derecognised, at which time the cumulative gain or loss previously recognised in equity is taken to the income statement, in the line that most appropriately reflects the nature of the item or transaction.

◆ Financial liabilities are also subdivided between those at fair value through profit and loss and those recorded at amortized cost.

Box 22.7 BT Group plc (2006) – Accounting policy note extract

Loans and other borrowings

Loans and other borrowings are initially recognised at fair value plus directly attributable transaction costs. Where loans and other borrowings contain a separable embedded derivative, the fair value of the embedded derivative is the difference between the fair value of the hybrid instrument and the fair value of the loan or borrowing. The fair value of the embedded derivative and the loan or borrowing is recorded separately on initial recognition. Loans and other borrowings are subsequently measured at amortised cost using the effective interest method and if included in a fair value hedge relationship are revalued to reflect the fair value movements on the hedged risk associated with the loans and other borrowings.

◆ Commercial hedging is a key component of the financial strategy of many large companies, and has historically been accompanied by specialized accounting treatment. The new accounting rules for hedge accounting are particularly demanding, and there is a strong feeling held by many within the accounting profession that it should eventually be eliminated. If all financial instruments were regularly marked to fair value and these movements recorded in the financial statements, hedge effectiveness would automatically be disclosed to the user.

FRS 26 (i.e. IAS 39) *Financial Instruments: Measurement* identifies three types of hedge.

1. **Fair value hedge:** The movements in the hedging instrument are used to offset the movements in the fair value of the instrument to be hedged. The movements on both items are taken direct to the profit and loss account.
2. **Cash flow hedge:** This is a hedge against the risk associated with the uncertainty of future cash flows. Consequently prior to settlement only one side of the hedge is known – the movement on the hedging instrument. These movements are taken to reserves until settlement when they can be recycled to the profit and loss account to offset gains or losses arising.

In practice not all of the movement on the hedging instrument may go to reserves as there are strict rules on hedge effectiveness. These require that the movements fall within a range of 80–125 per cent of the movements in the hedged item. When these boundaries are exceeded the arrangement is no longer deemed to be a hedge for accounting purposes. When the movement on the hedging instrument falls within the range but is not exactly 100 per cent then amounts in excess of this target will have to be taken directly to the profit and loss account.

3. **Net investment hedge**: This is a hedge against the exchange movements arising on net assets of an overseas operation and the accounting treatment is the same as for a cash flow hedge.

Box 22.8   Tate & Lyle plc (2006) – Accounting policy extract

(e) Commodity and treasury hedging instruments

Under IAS39, hedging relationships are categorized by type and must meet strict criteria to qualify for hedge accounting.

(i) Cash flow hedges

Hedges of firm commitments and highly probable forecast transactions, including forecast intra-group transactions that are expected to affect consolidated profit or loss, are designated as cash flow hedges. To the extent that movements in the fair values of these instruments effectively offset the underlying risk being hedged they are recognised in the hedging reserves in equity until the period during which the hedged forecast transaction affects profit or loss, at which point the cumulative gain or loss is recognised in the income statement, offsetting the value of the hedged transaction.

(ii) Fair value hedges

Hedges against the movement in fair value of recognised assets and liabilities are designated as fair value hedges. To the extent that movements in the fair values of these instruments effectively offset the underlying risk being hedged they are recognised in the income statement by offset against the hedged transaction.

(iii) Hedges of net investments

Hedges of a net investment in a foreign operation are designated as net investment hedges. To the extent that movements in the fair values of these instruments effectively offset the underlying risk being hedged they are recognised in the translation reserve until the period during which a foreign operation is disposed of or partially disposed of, at which point the cumulative gain or loss is recognised in profit or loss, offsetting the cumulative difference recognised on the translation of the net investment.

Hedge accounting is discontinued at the point when the hedging instrument no longer qualifies for hedge accounting. In the case of cash flow hedging relationships, the cumulative movement in the fair value of the hedging instrument previously recognised in equity up to that point is retained there until the forecast transaction affects profit or loss, unless the hedged transaction is no longer expected to occur, in which case the cumulative movement in fair value is transferred to profit or loss immediately. Movements in the fair value of hedging instruments where the instrument failed to meet the IAS39 hedge accounting criteria or where the movement represents the ineffective portion of a qualifying hedging relationship are recognised in the income statement immediately as other income and expense or net finance expense, as appropriate.

Main sources of guidance

UK GAAP

- Companies Act 1985
- FRS 20 *Share-based Payment*
- FRS 21 *Events after the Balance Sheet Date*
- FRS 22 *Earnings per Share*
- FRS 23 *The Effects of Changes in Foreign Exchange Rates*
- FRS 24 *Financial Reporting in Hyperinflationary Economies*
- FRS 25 *Financial Instruments: Disclosure and Presentation*
- FRS 26 *Financial Instruments: Measurement*
- FRS 29 *Financial Instrument: Disclosures*.

International GAAP

- ◆ IFRS 2 *Share-based Payment*
- ◆ IAS 10 *Events after the Balance Sheet Date*
- ◆ IAS 33 *Earnings per Share*
- ◆ IAS 21 *The Effects of Changes in Foreign Exchange Rates*
- ◆ IAS 29 *Financial Reporting in Hyperinflationary Economies*
- ◆ IAS 32 *Financial Instruments: Disclosure and Presentation*
- ◆ IAS 39 *Financial Instruments: Measurement*
- ◆ IFRS 7 *Financial Instrument: Disclosures.*

Key Facts

1. UK GAAP is progressively becoming international GAAP as new ASB accounting standards represent the adoption of their international counterparts.
2. The only UK companies who are currently exempted from the new UK standards are those using the FRSSE (Financial Reporting Standard for Smaller Entities).
3. The progressive adoption of international accounting practice into UK GAAP should not be confused with the full adoption of international GAAP by listed companies for the preparation of their group financial statements.
4. At the date of publication the incorporation of international practice into UK GAAP had incorporated the following subjects:
   - ◆ Share-based payment – most prevalent for employee benefits such as options, resulting in a charge being raised against profits from the grant date to the vesting date.
   - ◆ Events after the balance-sheet date – the most significant change arising from this adoption is that dividends must be recognized in the accounting period when they are declared.
   - ◆ Earnings per share – modest changes in detail but for the average user little has changed.
   - ◆ Foreign currency – the international rules should lead to improved inter-company comparison as the number of allowed alternative treatments has been significantly reduced. It also introduces the new terms 'functional' and 'presentational currency'.
   - ◆ Hyperinflationary economies – Again a reduction of accepted accounting treatments from two to one. The remaining

methodology based on adjusting by the movements in a general price index.

◆ Financial instruments – a two-pronged attack on this complex subject with increased disclosure and a requirement to measure and recognize the instruments on the balance sheet. Some aspects of the guidance remain controversial and it is probable that further amendments and guidance will continue to be developed.

Flicking the Switch:
First-time Adoption

Setting expectations

Making the switch from long-established local accounting rules to a new regime in one jump is a considerable task for any entity irrespective of the resources available to it. The IASB recognized the challenge and to assist transition issued an accounting standard bespoke to this issue: IFRS 1 *First-time Adoption of IFRS*. The opening paragraph of this standard makes it clear that the first financial statements (including interim financial statements for that period) produced under the new rules must contain high quality information that:

◆ is transparent for users and comparable over all periods presented;
◆ provides a suitable starting point for accounting under IFRS; and
◆ can be generated at a cost that does not exceed the benefits to users.

[IFRS 1 para 1]

For UK companies the basic rules of transition are covered in Chapter 2, and can be distilled to the following:

1. Companies with debt or equity listed on a regulated exchange within the EU must produce IFRS-compliant group financial statements for their accounting periods starting on or after 1 January 2005.
2. Adjustments arising from the transfer are to be taken to reserves and not through the face of the profit and loss account.
3. Partial transfer is not allowed; there must be full adoption of IFRS rules.

In the light of the implementation date the relevance of IFRS 1 may seem spurious, but it is important to be aware of the impact international accounting had on the financial position and performance of a business, particularly when considering long-term trends.

Additional disclosures

The transition to a new set of accounting rules results in the derecognition of some assets and liabilities, recognition of others for the first time and changes in both classification and disclosure. If a user of the financial statements is to understand these changes additional disclosures are required in the first IFRS-compliant financial statements.

IFRS 1 requires two key reconciliations to have been disclosed:

1. A reconciliation of equity both at the date of transition and the end of the latest period presented in the entity's most recent annual financial statements prepared under previous GAAP.
2. A reconciliation of profit and loss reported under previous accounting rules.

Box 23.1   Halfords plc (2006) – UK GAAP to IFRS reconciliation

25. Reconciliation of net assets and profit under UK GAAP to IFRS

The Group reported under UK GAAP in its published financial statements for the 52 weeks to 1 April 2005. The analysis below shows a reconciliation of net assets and profit as reported under UK GAAP for the 52 weeks to 1 April 2005 to the revised net assets and profit under IFRS as reported in these financial statements. In addition, there is a reconciliation of net assets under UK GAAP to IFRS at the transition date for the Group being 3 April 2004.

Key impacts

The main impacts of IFRS on the reported results of the Group are listed below and are described in greater detail in the following sections.

◆ **Goodwill (IFRS 3)** — Acquired goodwill should no longer be amortised and is instead subjected to an annual impairment review. At the date of transition to IFRS the value of goodwill is frozen.

◆ **Share Based Payments (IFRS 2)** — Fair value based charges are required for all awards made for share schemes on or after 7 November 2002 which had not vested by 2 April 2005.

◆ **Property Leases (IAS 17)** — The building element of the lease relating to the Group's head office in Redditch has been reclassified as a finance lease. Lease incentives must now be amortised in the income statement over the lease term not to the date of the first rent review.

◆ **Timing and Recognition of Dividends (IAS 10)** — Final dividends declared after the Balance Sheet date cannot be recognised at the Balance Sheet date and instead are reported in the period in which they are approved.

- ◆ **Intangible Assets (IAS 38)** — Software costs previously categorised within tangible fixed assets must now be shown as intangible assets in the Balance Sheet.

	52 weeks to 1 April 2005 £ m
Operating profit under UK GAAP as previously reported	78.3
Prior year adjustment — rebates	(1.3)
Operating profit under UK GAAP restated	77.0
Goodwill amortisation	13.7
Share-based payment	(1.0)
Reclassification of assets from operating to finance leases	0.4
Lease incentives	(0.8)
IFRS adjustments	12.3
Operating profit under IFRS	89.3

	1 April 2005 £m
Net assets under UK GAAP as previously reported	156.3
Prior year adjustment — rebates	(3.9)
Net assets under UK GAAP restated	152.4
Goodwill amortization	13.7
Holiday pay accrual	(0.5)
Reclassification of assets from operating to finance leases	(0.5)
Lease incentives	(6.4)
Tax on above adjustments	(1.9)
Dividend recognition	18.9
IFRS adjustments	23.3
Net assets under IFRS	175.7

Reconciliation of the income statement for the 52 weeks to 1 April 2005

	Ref	UK GAAP 2005 £m	IFRS 2005 £m	Difference £m
Revenue		628.4	628.4	–
Cost of sales	1.1	(290.7)	(292.0)	(1.3)
Gross profit		337.7	336.4	(1.3)
Operating expenses	1.2	(259.4)	(247.1)	12.3
Operating profit		78.3	89.3	11.0
Net finance costs	1.3	(14.2)	(15.0)	(0.8)
Profit before tax		64.1	74.3	10.2
Taxation	1.4	(24.2)	(23.2)	1.0
Profit attributable to equity shareholders		39.9	51.1	11.2
Basic EPS (pence)		18.5p	23.7p	5.2p

The differences upon the profit attributable to equity shareholders are:

	2005 £m
Reference 1.1 **Cost of sales**	
Prior year adjustment to "Inventories": an adjustment has been made for a UK GAAP error to absorb an appropriate portion of rebate income into the cost of inventories, which was previously recognised as received in the income statement.	(1.3)
Reference 1.2 **Operating expenses**	2005 £m
IFRS 2 "Share-based payment" requires the assignment of fair values at the date of grant to the options granted to employees after 7 November 2002 which had not vested by 2 April 2005. The expense is spread over the vesting period of these options.	(1.0)

IAS 17 **"Leases"** results in the reclassification of the head office building from being held as an operating lease to a finance lease. The asset has been depreciated over the useful economic life and the interest associated with the lease reclassified from operating expenses to finance costs.   0.4

IAS 17 **"Leases"** requires the release of lease incentives over the life of the lease rather than over the period to the first rent review. Consequently, there has been a reduction in the release of lease incentives from the balance sheet.   (0.8)

IFRS 3 "Business combinations" requires the non-amortisation of goodwill arising on business combinations. Under UK GAAP goodwill was amortised over 20 years.   13.7

	12.3

Reference 1.3	2005
Net finance costs	£m

IAS 17 **"Leases"** resulted in the reclassification of the head office building from an operating to a finance lease. The interest associated with the lease has been reclassified from operating expenses to finance costs.   (0.8)

Reference 1.4	2005
Taxation	£m

IAS 12 **"Income taxes"** resulted in the recognition of a deferred tax liability regarding assets acquired in prior periods that did not qualify for capital allowances. This deferred tax liability has been released as follows: 0.8

IAS 17 **"Leases"** led to the creation of deferred tax assets relating to lease premiums that were not previously accounted for under UK GAAP. The movement on the deferred tax asset has been as follows: 0.1

IAS 19 **"Employee benefits"** led to the recognition of a deferred tax asset for employee holiday pay.   0.1

	1.0

Reconciliation of equity at 1 April 2005 and 3 April 2004 (Date of transition to IFRS)

	Ref	UK GAAP 2005 £m	IFRS 2005 £m	Difference £m	UK GAAP 2004 £m	IFRS 2004 £m	Difference £m
Non-current assets							
Goodwill	2.1	239.4	253.1	13.7	253.1	253.1	–
Intangible assets	2.2	–	6.2	6.2	–	3.0	3.0
Property, plant and equipment	2.3	91.8	97.8	6.0	82.5	92.2	9.7
		331.2	357.1	25.9	335.6	348.3	12.7
Current assets							
Inventories	2.4	112.2	108.3	(3.9)	107.1	104.5	(2.6)
Trade and other receivables		23.6	23.6	–	23.5	23.5	–
Cash and cash equivalents		1.1	1.1	–	25.6	25.6	–
		136.9	133.0	(3.9)	156.2	153.6	(2.6)
Current liabilities							
Borrowings	2.5	(52.1)	(52.2)	(0.1)	(189.4)	(189.5)	(0.1)
Trade and other payables	2.6	(117.7)	(99.3)	18.4	(94.3)	(94.8)	(0.5)
Current tax liabilities		(13.3)	(13.3)	–	(10.1)	(10.1)	–
Provisions		(1.6)	(1.6)	–	(1.0)	(1.0)	–
		(184.7)	(166.4)	18.3	(294.8)	(295.4)	(0.6)
Net current liabilities		(47.8)	(33.4)	14.4	(138.6)	(141.8)	(3.2)

Non-current liabilities

	Note	2005			2004		
		£m	£m	£m	£m	£m	£m
Borrowings	2.7	(118.7)	(131.3)	(12.6)	(185.6)	(198.2)	(12.6)
Deferred tax liabilities	2.8	(3.2)	(5.1)	(1.9)	(2.3)	(5.2)	(2.9)
Other non-current liabilities	2.9	(5.2)	(11.6)	(6.4)	(4.6)	(10.3)	(5.7)
		(127.1)	(148.0)	(20.9)	(192.5)	(213.7)	(21.2)
Net assets		**156.3**	**175.7**	**19.4**	**4.5**	**(7.2)**	**(11.7)**
Equity							
Share capital		**2.3**	**2.3**	—	—	—	—
Share premium		**132.9**	**132.9**	—	**0.1**	**0.1**	—
Retained earnings	2.10	**21.1**	**40.5**	**19.4**	**4.4**	**(7.3)**	**(11.7)**
Total equity		**156.3**	**175.7**	**19.4**	**4.5**	**(7.2)**	**(11.7)**

The differences are explained as follows:

Reference 2.1

	2005 £m	2004 £m
Goodwill	**13.7**	—

IFRS 3 **"Business combinations"** resulted in the write-back of goodwill previously amortised since the transition date of 3 April 2004.

Reference 2.2

	2005 £m	2004 £m
Intangible assets	**6.2**	**3.0**

IAS 38 **"Intangible assets"** requires the reclassification of software development costs from property, plant and equipment to intangible fixed assets.

Reference 2.3

Property, plant and equipment	2005 £m	2004 £m
	12.2	**12.7**
	(6.2)	**(3.0)**
	6.0	**9.7**

IAS 17 **"Leases"** resulted in the reclassification of a building from an operating lease to a finance lease. The asset is being depreciated over its useful economic life.
IAS 38 **"Intangible assets"** requires the reclassification of software development costs from property, plant and equipment to intangible fixed assets.

	2005 £m	2004 £m
Reference 2.4 **Inventories**		

Prior year adjustment to "Inventories": an adjustment has been made for a UK GAAP error to absorb an appropriate portion of rebate income into inventories. which was previously recognised in the Income Statement.

	2005 £m	2004 £m
	(3.9)	(2.6)
Reference 2.5 **Borrowings**		

IAS 17 "Leases" results in the reclassification of a lease relating to the head office building which was formerly held as an operating lease as a finance lease.

	2005 £m	2004 £m
	(0.1)	(0.1)
Reference 2.6 **Trade and other payables**		

IAS 37 **"Provisions, contingent liabilities and contingent assets"** requires that dividends are recognised in the period in which they are approved.

IAS 19 **"Employee benefits"** requires the recognition of holiday pay due to and from employees. A liability arises at the year end due to employees carrying forward accrued benefits to the following financial year.

	2005 £m	2004 £m
	18.9	–
	(0.5)	(0.5)
	18.4	(0.5)
Reference 2.7 **Borrowings**		

IAS 17 **"Leases"** results in the recognition of a building as a finance lease, which was formerly held as an operating lease (see note 2.3).

	2005 £m	2004 £m
	(12.6)	(12.6)
Reference 2.8 **Deferred income tax liabilities**		

IAS 12 **"Income taxes"** results in the recognition of a deferred tax liability regarding assets acquired in prior periods that did not qualify for capital allowances.

	2005 £m	2004 £m
	(4.0)	(4.8)

	2005 £m	2004 £m
IAS 17 "Leases" leads to the creation of deferred tax assets relating to lease incentives.	**1.9**	1.7
IAS 19 "Employee benefits" led to the recognition of a deferred tax asset for employee holiday pay.	**0.2**	0.2
	(1.9)	(2.9)

Reference 2.9
Other non-current liabilities

	2005 £m	2004 £m
The adoption of **IAS 17 "Leases"** results in the profit on the sale of a property being reclassified as deferred income rather than being recognised in the Income Statement. The effect on deferred income was:	**(3.6)**	(3.7)
The adoption of **IAS 17 "Leases"** requires the release of lease incentives over the life of the lease rather than over the period to the first rent review. Consequently, there has been a reduction in the release of lease incentives from the Balance Sheet. The effect on deferred income was:	**(2.8)**	(2.0)
	(6.4)	(5.7)

Reference 2.10
Retained earnings

	2005 £m	2004 £m
The adoption of IFRS and the UK GAAP error had the following net impact on retained earnings. Cumulative total of all adjustments to the Balance Sheet was:	**19.4**	(11.7)

Reconciliation of the Consolidated Cash Flow Statements
The principal difference between UK GAAP and IFRS in the Group's statement of cash flow is the reconciliation to cash and bank overdrafts rather than net debt (which included bank loans and finance lease creditors).

Exemptions

IFRS 1 recognized that in a limited number of circumstances it was not practical to ask first-time adopters to comply with the exactitudes of certain standards as the cost of so doing would outweigh the benefit to a potential user of the resultant financial statements. To this end the standard incorporates a modest number of optional or mandatory exemptions.

By taking advantage of these exemptions an entity will influence its future financial statements (i.e. the ones you are looking at now), and hence they do have a prospective relevance. Particularly noteworthy in this context are the following.

Business combinations

Business combinations prior to the transition from UK GAAP and accounted for using merger accounting rules did not have to be reclassified in spite of the fact that merger accounting is prohibited under international GAAP.

Fair value

Fair value at the date of transition or a revaluation made under UK GAAP could be treated as deemed cost. This negated the need for ongoing revaluations.

Employee benefits

The 10 per cent-corridor approach could be adopted prospectively from the date of transition without the need to look prior to the transition in an attempt to calculate a value for actuarial gains and losses that would not yet have been recognized via the profit and loss account.

Foreign exchange translation differences

Unlike international GAAP the foreign exchange differences taken to the reserves when using the net investment method did not have to be recycled to the profit and loss account upon the disposal of the investment. The exemption allowed the cumulative exchange difference to be set to zero at the date of transition.

Some of the exemptions in IFRS 1 were mandatory, in particular requirements that the use of hindsight could not be used to revise estimates, and that financial assets and liabilities derecognized prior to 1 January 2004 could not be recognized on the opening IFRS balance sheet.

Other exemptions related to subjects such as compound financial instruments, hedge accounting and timing issues relating to the adoption of IFRS by associates and joint ventures.

Main sources of guidance

International GAAP

♦ IFRS 1 First-time adoption of IFRS

Key facts

1. With the exception of a small number of exemptions IFRS 1 requires entities transferring from local to international GAAP to make the transition in one step.
2. Mandatory reconciliations for profit and loss and equity are required by the standard to ensure the impact of the transition can be understood by stakeholders.

Index